SURVIVING THE
COMFORT ZONE

SURVIVING THE COMFORT ZONE

By Roy Masters

Edited by Dorothy Baker

Surviving the Comfort Zone
©1991 by Roy Masters
Published by the Foundation of Human Understanding

The Foundation of Human Understanding
PO Box 1009
Grants Pass, OR 97526
(800) 877-3227

Printed in the United States of America

Library of Congress Catalog No. 91-073149

ISBN # 0-933900-15-5

Contents

Introduction

LOVE. It is one of the most commonly used words in the English language—and one of the most   powerful. From childhood we yearn for love because it holds such great promise of happiness, fulfillment, and permanence. As we get older, the popular culture tells us "love is all you need," but we soon learn the "needing" never really stops. The emptiness in our lives that we keep trying to fill never really gets filled, not by spouse, lover, friend, career, possession, pet, or whatever else we turn to for comfort.

Sometimes, we think we've found something that will make us happy, but then the pain of longing comes back *stronger than ever*. No matter what we do, the "hot and cold" moods of desire and frustration seem to haunt us, until we start to think it's the normal way to be. But we know it's not.

The braver ones of us can face this, and start looking for real answers, but most people try to soothe the pain any way they can. And there are plenty of people ready to help—for a price. Drugs, alcohol, cigarettes are the usual methods, but for all the public focus on these, there are more common escapes—possibly more dangerous—like movies and television, sex, or even music if used the wrong way. And when it comes to *surviving the comfort zone*, there is no greater temptation than *food*.

All these things supply love—not true love, but a kind of *comfort love*, or ego support. We are vulnerable to this substitute for the real thing because most of us don't know what the real thing is. So, we reach out for what's available. And we're miserable.

After years of pain, however, more and more people are starting to realize there's something wrong with what is commonly called "love." Family lives that are supposed to be filled with love are often living nightmares that leave children feeling helpless, fearful, and alone in the world. Fathers and mothers have forgotten who they are—to their children and to each other. Most marriages have more to do with sex than love, and so, the divorce rate skyrockets.

After years of following the popular culture, people are lost, and growing numbers are desperate to understand where they went wrong. Today's youth, increasingly damaged by premature sexual relationships and misguided attitudes, are quietly asking themselves, "If this is love, why does it feel like *dying*?"

Anyone who hungers for answers to that question may find it within these pages.

—Robert Just

1

Users: The Hate that Masquerades as Love

We use the word "love" to refer to two distinctly different emotions, although most of us are completely unaware of the distinction between pure love and the impostor for the simple reason that the impostor "love" is the only love we have ever known.

For love to be pure, of course, it can not be adulterated by any emotion or consideration of advantage on the part of the bestower. It is the love I frequently refer to as "not hate"; for strictly speaking, pure love is not an emotion at all. It is simply a selfless obedience to God's will, to what we intuitively know to be the right thing to do. Pure love would be impossible for an atheist to experience, depending as it does on complete submission to an authority higher than our own egos. This phenomenon (I can hardly call it an emotion) of pure love, rarely as it is to be encountered in our materialistic society, is nevertheless the very *modus operandi* of the pure in heart, of those who have arrived at the state of objectivity that I hope to guide all of you to through the meditation exercise.

In the meantime, let's take a closer look at the love that grows out of hate (resentment). Strangely enough, the very situation that calls out for love also evokes and serves to justify the reaction of hate in those who have never known real love. All the situations that "try men's souls" are "trying" or challenging only because we have no love with which to meet them.

The "love" we have grown up on, the only love most of us have ever known, is a love that grew out of hate. Needless to say, such love is always false, violent, violating, and destructive. And it is the love that passes from one generation to the next through the failure of our parents, and of their parents before them, to resist the temptation to hate. Once we give in to the pull of resentment, we cut ourselves off from the true ground of our being, and pride rushes in to support and transform us.

This new self, feeling the pain and guilt of its separation from God, must now turn to its new god for comfort, to the loveless, impatient spirit of the man or woman who corrupted it. That is why all men are literally looking for their mothers in their wives; and all women seek their fathers in their husbands. There is no escape. They can be attracted only to those persons in whom they can find the familiar spirit of their parents.

Once the transformation has taken place, the changeling is forced to resolve its conflict with God in Pride's way; that is, by rejecting any lingering guilt for having strayed from God's truth through reaching out to "people" truth and its emotion-sustaining false love.

When we resent a parent, we create within ourselves a need for that parent's acceptance; and we need that acceptance, not only from the actual parent, but also from the parent equivalent we have found in the husband, wife, friend/fiend, or dope pusher. While true love is a crying out for the nurturing source of creation, false love is a crying need for the source of its corruption. The displaced identity cries out for the embrace of the very hell that caused it to come into existence through hatred.

An unloved woman loves out of guilt or hate, and she expresses that love for her family by supporting them in their weakness and thus spoiling them to death. She falls all over herself to please a man in order to conceal and soothe the secret loathing she feels for all men. She services his need in order to service her own need to judge. A large part of this hatred of all men does not grow out of a woman's own experience, but is an inheritance from her mother. A girl child soon learns to hate her father because her mother hates him. She simply feels what her mother feels because she is bonded to her mother in such a way that she feels what her mother feels for her husband. In this way, all women unconsciously inherit contempt for all men, and they "love" them in order to bring them down to a level where their pride can feed on them and grow fat with hate and judgment. Thus, we humans persist in violating one another, not only through overt hatred, but through the covert form of it that we foolishly call "love."

Man, as Scripture records, was seduced originally by a sympathetic love for his rebellious ego; and to this day, man is addicted to supportive love to kill the anxiety he would otherwise feel over what he has become through "love." Woman, on the other hand, seduced by the promise of an ungodly power, has used it to feed her resentment of all the men in her life, beginning with her father, who have broken their covenant with God and have come down to need her. In other words, a woman knows that she must betray a man with phony, ego-stroking "love" in order to gain his acceptance; and men can't help but betray the women in their lives because they have fallen from the allegiance to God that would have guaranteed their allegiance to real love.

Man's craven need to use woman in the name of "love" in order to complete his ego identity has caused him to become addicted to the false, lying love of a woman. But this craven need to use is actually a misdirected cry for God, and when woman answers the cry, she becomes the dominant "creative" power in the relationship. The ego/pride in man born of woman cries out to its origin to be nurtured. Little does the male child, the changeling, realize what he is calling out to in the agony of his need. It is the dark side of woman that was present in Eve on the day she fled the garden. This dark principle has survived her flesh to soothe and nurture the generations of fallen men who, by love, continue to fall again and again, only to become the objects of her hate, forced by guilt to masquerade as love. This condescending love, based on contempt, is the only love most women have ever known.

So it has come to pass that while man comes down to evolve his pride through the process of falling in "love," woman, being corrupted by her judgment (hatred) of man's need, falls in *hate* and becomes addicted to loving men as an escape from desolation, despair, emptiness, and loneliness of soul—perhaps also out of a need for revenge, draining man of power to get back at him for his use of her. Thus "loving" destroys man and woman alike. Woman fixes her need for loathing by fixing man's need for loving. Hers is a judgment fix; his is a love fix.

While man was seduced originally by the understanding and compassionate Eve, and while he still seeks her out to spoil him rotten with reinforcing sex, man can also be corrupted by the hatred he feels toward emerging female dominance.

The first rage a man feels is toward his father, either for his not having been man enough to stand up to his mother, or for the excessive force he used to have his way with her. Like the female child, the male child feels what all women feel toward all husbands. It is the sin of unconscious hate for his father that not only separates him from the true ground of his male identity, but also makes it impossible for him ever to find God again.

In other words, by rejecting the father he can see, he also rejects the Father that he cannot see. In the process, he also rejects his own true identity. Now, by hating his father, he unconsciously accepts his mother's nature and sets himself up to need a woman's love in order to complete and reaffirm the identity she has given him. It is his reaching out for love that puts pressure on every woman in his life to give him the kind of love that will destroy them both in the end.

Resentment toward the father has a somewhat different effect on the female child. Where the male child becomes love-needful, the female child becomes hate-needful. She becomes a man hater and man *eater,* provoking and teasing for *real* love and becoming resentful and frustrated by the unhealthy sex attention men give her in its place. The contempt she feels satisfies her ego need to judge, but the guilt of that judgment sets her up to allow herself to be used. She then proceeds to indulge herself in hating the user. While killing whatever might have been lying dormant of the man's original God-given identity, the dark spirit in her munches on his remains.

Women tend to select weak, wimpy, or violent men as mates, since both extremes embody the particular failing she needs for the evolution of the pride that entered her through hate, via man's fall from original love. But false love, the one that rises out of hate through guilt (the one mother feels for father) is the only "love" most women have ever known, hate having separated them once and for all from realizing the painful truth about such love. Because love and truth are one, to lose one is to lose the other. Female love is the font from which all men drink themselves into a drunken stupor, so that they too become separated from the knowledge of truth.

Fallen men continue to see women as the source of love and worship. They look to the female body for the renewal of their fallen spirits. Their egos tell them that "this must be love because it feels so good"; but in the fullness of time, the friction that is bound to flare up between "users" may wake man to the truth of his fallen condition, if he will only listen.

The hate/love relationship between man and woman has a counterpart in the relationship between the addict and the pusher. The addict, like the man, has the illusion that he is coming into his kingdom, whereas he is slowly becoming a derelict and a pauper. And just as the pusher depends on the addict's downfall for his livelihood, the woman exploits man's inherent weakness to feed her own unconscious habit, her love of hate. And just as the addict is dependent on the pusher for the *illusion* of power, so is the pusher dependent on the addict for *actual* power. Of such is the kingdom of hell.

Men make women into hags to feed in them a hunger that can never be satisfied. And the women changelings, hags, feel falsely secure in their hate. Out of the contempt such women feel comes hell's love. Men and women can not live *with* each other or *without* each other, for each has built his false identity on the destruction of the other. Wretched man-eaters and woman-eaters that we are, only God, through the love of His son, can save us.

Hate is the emotion that supports the judgment side of pride, while "love" soothes the pain of the hate and supports the God-supplanting side of pride. All imitators of God reserve to themselves the power and rights of God. In a perverse way we are all kings and judges. To play god, our pride needs a patsy whose ego can be puffed up to such a ridiculous size that it practically asks to be judged, and we are all too glad to oblige. The feelings of omnipotence conjured up by "love" spring from a lie, but so does the hate that follows; for when we see how the loves we have called upon have betrayed, enslaved, and enfeebled us, we hate and judge in order to avoid facing the truth.

The fallen ego, in its rebellion against God to be its own god, is sustained by two emotions: we call one of them "love" (it isn't) and the other "hate" (more accurately, resentment). And the love that rises out of resentment can never really get off the ground, but flops back and forth endlessly between the "love" that is hate and the hate that is hate. In the coupling of two egos, neither one can ever emerge a winner, for the pride they both serve leads inevitably to anxiety, guilt, violence, mental illness, all manner of tragedy, and ultimately, death.

Love spawned of hate is the emotion of selfishness, and it sustains every vile quirk of our personality—everything that has gone wrong with us since our first flash of resentment opened the door to pride, the corrupter. As long as we have a "lover," we have a "savior," and what he or she saves us from is the ordeal of facing ourselves as we are, and repenting of what we see in the mirror of truth.

The movies have made popular a definition of love as "never having to say you're sorry," but that kind of love is a lie. It leads to the loathing that leads to the need for "loving" that leads to the need for loathing, again and again, until loving and loathing are seen to be one and the same. Destination: death.

"Love" consoles its prey, and it accomplishes its deception through the emotional involvement of its victim. How can a fallen ego possibly avoid falling in love with the tempter to whom all its obvious faults are acceptable and "only natural"? In this context, falling in love is a glorious escape from the truth and the pain of repentance, which is the price we must pay for true salvation. As long as we are willing to lap up the lie that all our flaws of character are normal and natural, we fail to question our false belief systems, and thus we sink ever deeper into the quagmire of emotion, "safe" from the astringent demands of reality.

Adam doubted God and became wrong, and then he needed Eve to help him doubt that he was wrong for having doubted God. And just in case he really *was* wrong, he needed her to blame, not only for that but for anything else that might go wrong in their lives. What a neat trick! How easy it is to preserve an air of innocence when there is someone around to blame for every mishap. Our unwillingness to admit that we are wrong leads us to project our wrong onto the innocent; and they, perceiving the injustice of our accusation, are tempted to hate, thus falling to sin—innocent no more. Once we learn this easy way to project guilt, we become addicted to blaming others in order to free ourselves from the redeeming pain of conscience and go on our merry, wicked way.

By now, my women readers must see how important it is for them to forgive their fathers and husbands for their weakness, for by loathing male needfulness women turn their backs on innocence and begin to operate entirely from the dark side of their psyche. How many more generations of proud, hate-based mutants can this country assimilate and still call itself the land of the free? It also behooves my men readers to take a good look at their propensity for being attracted to women who loathe them.

A man should not look on his marriage license as an *open sesame* to unlimited sex. He should forbear to touch his wife at all if he sees that she is reacting strangely to his advances. Obviously, such a woman has a problem where sex is concerned. She may have been raped or molested by her father or some other member of the family; somehow, she has come to associate sex with abusive use, and she will hate any man for using her selfishly, even if you are not (which is highly unlikely). If you lack the patience to wait until the problem can be resolved through your joint efforts, but persist in forcing the issue, any "love" she gives you from that point on will be based on hate. Out of her hatred for all mankind she will be obligated to submit to sexual abuse in order to feed her need to judge—to be powerful, omnipotent. Remember that the ego need of a woman who has been violated has come into existence through the cruelty of men. Or through her father's failing to be there for her and thus save her from her mother. All women share a resentment for the weak men who attract them and who serve as food for their judgment.

Let us all beware the love that has its roots in resentment.

2

She Stoops to Conquer

Have you noticed that the world in general is run by dull stupid people? The more inferior a person is, the more likely he is to gravitate to a position of power. It is as though society just can't do enough for its obsequious dummies, but must reward them with one position of authority after another, each one greater than the last. At least, that is the way the system works as long as the dummy plays the game and keeps trying to be all things to all people. Should he suddenly wake up and start to rock the boat—well, that's another story entirely.

Similarly, a man will be so pleased to find a sweet, submissive, non-threatening little woman (crazy like a fox) to idolize him that before he knows what hit him, he will have given her complete control over all that he has; worse yet, over all that he is. He loves the feeling of mastery he gets from her deference to his every wish and thought. He may even look on her support and adulation as his God-given due; after all, she is "only" a woman, and therefore she is only too glad to do everything in her power for the superior person he thinks he is. That is the way he sees it, or tries to.

In his lucid moments, he has to see that for all her adulation and supportiveness, she is the dominant person in the relationship. When he first becomes aware of the subtle dichotomy between the way things appear to be and the way they really are, he might try very hard to build himself up by putting her down, but no matter how hard he may try, she always emerges dominant. Even when she puts herself down, apologizing for her stupidity and helplessness, she still comes out on top, and this can be very frustrating to the male ego.

The fact of the matter is that it's hard to score a clear victory over the person who is not only supporting your ego, but is also hiding under it. Women seem to know almost instinctively that when you make yourself small with people you give them the illusion that they are great, and they will love you for that effect. It is a kind of survival tool for a woman in a man's world.

Women, like politicians, know that they must present themselves as willing tools to those who have elected them to serve. That is, they must do so if they hope to gain any power for themselves. Unfortunately, the power they often gain is the power to confuse, diminish, and destroy the man they are "serving."

Guileful women love to play "dumb," and many of them become so skillful at it that you never know how much is "for real" and how much is simply their way of outsmarting you. For instance, you may say something that you think to be quite clever, only to be met by a kind of glazed-over uncomprehending expression that you can take to mean that she failed to understand you; on the other hand, it can just as well mean that your clever remark is going over with a dull thud because it wasn't all that clever.

And you know that no matter how hard you may push the issue, she isn't about to level with you because she is having too much fun watching you squirm on the horns of your dilemma, your confusion over being unable to find the appropriate response because you are not quite sure what it is you are trying to respond to. Even when she seems to capitulate and agree with you, you get the distinct impression that she is doing so only to make you happy and keep the peace. If you are a stickler for truth, you don't want peace at that price. In fact, you might start leaning more toward violence. Or sex. Frustration often ends that way.

Why, you might ask, would a woman want to play dumb; or why, when she was born as intelligent as any man, would she submit to reducing her conscious awareness in a man's presence? The answer is that she learns to give up intelligence in exchange for power. A woman knows that when she appears to be somewhat lacking in awareness, vulnerable, easy to take advantage of, her appeal to a man's ego and sexuality will be almost irresistible. The woman who makes herself blind to her husband's faults is very sexy indeed, and male egos like that.

The trouble with such an arrangement is that every time a man's ego gets such a boost, he becomes less of a human being, a fact which, when it finally dawns on him, will enrage him. At that point, no matter how much the woman blinds herself to his weaknesses, she can never make him truly happy. In fact, her efforts to make him happy seem destined to render him ever *less* happy. So now the pressure is on her to submit and make him happy. The responsibility is enormous. It is also a killer.

Playing dumb, as I remarked earlier, is being crazy like a fox, for into the emptiness of a vacated consciousness slinks a dark manipulative intelligence that now teaches the woman how to become dumber than ever, less aware of the man's faults, and therefore more supportive and submissive (dominant). Men traditionally see such women as *loving* and *understanding*. But, like it or not, such a woman gradually becomes the ground of man's devolving being, the rug that can be pulled out from under his feet; and a man caught in the trap of building his life on such a "dumb-waiter" relationship is in mortal danger.

The more he tries to put the woman down in order to delude himself into thinking that he is the boss, the more pliable and insecure he becomes. Why? Because an ego that can get high on an outside buildup is doomed to fall. Now, the "fox" part of the "crazy" begins to emerge and make demands. "God! This stupid little bitch is in control of my life," he thinks to himself. So he tries harder to put her down and belittle her, only to come out the loser over and over again. He can't win for losing, and it was for this ungodly power that the woman traded in her natural claim to intelligence.

A woman who, for one reason or another, hates her own femininity whenever she has to relate to a man (usually because the men close to her have put her down all her life) will often be surprisingly adept at playing the dumb submissive role. She uses it, of course, as a means of getting revenge against the kinds of characters (any man becomes a stand-in for all of them) who have deprived her of any joy she might have known had she been able to accept herself as the woman she was meant to be.

She may not fully realize how completely she is destroying the man by giving him the kind of love he demands of her—at least, not in the beginning—because she thinks she is operating out of weakness; but she soon discovers that she has all the aces, all the power. And the poor man might not even know he is being had. After all, she is giving him the only kind of love a man demands of a woman; in order to live with him at all she has to kill him with love. But this kind of love is from the pit, the dark side of the force. Being ego supportive, it takes away a man's shame and frees him to indulge his senses however he sees fit. He feels like a god, but he is becoming a monkey.

We might see more honesty and integrity in man/woman relationships were it not for the unremitting strength of *male sexual pressure,* which produces the kind of love that leads to the egotistical jockeying for power we've been discussing. A woman doesn't have to be very old before it deprives her of her girlish innocence and causes her to hate men. When she falls to the pressure, the pure love she once knew for what is noble and good devolves into a deceitful love for what is wicked and selfish. She can't lick them, so she joins them, and is rewarded by the selfish men she serves with all kinds of material things and favors that she would be unlikely to obtain by her own efforts.

Before long, the only kind of love a woman knows how to give is the only kind of love a man wants. If she were somehow to wake up and recapture her innocence long enough to become aware of the man's faults, her awareness would drive him into a rage; he couldn't stand to see himself by her light. His feelings of shame, awkwardness, and embarrassment would simply be too much for him. He would feel that she had somehow betrayed him; he would feel perfectly justified in going out to find someone more "compatible." It is fairly easy for him to do, of course, as the world is full of deceiving witches, and he will soon find the unprincipled kind of woman he so richly deserves.

Of course, if it were the other way around, and the man woke up to the damage they were doing with their game playing, the woman would feel just as threatened, but she would be more inclined to persevere in her witchery for the sake of keeping the marriage together.

So it comes to pass that a woman becomes addicted to a life of deception, either to enjoy the power it gives her or simply to hang onto the security of the family relationship, to keep the peace. But there is no peace. Not in her. Not in him. She can't keep him happy without making herself miserable and inferior. She must forever blind herself to his evolving faults and his many indiscretions. She must become, or at least *seem* to become, less and less conscious so that he can go on thinking he is on the people end of the leash, when in reality he is just the puppy dog panting for her favors.

Even when a woman becomes aware, as they sometimes do, of a dark self emerging from the depths of her soul, even when she is aware that the spirit of her man is loving and embracing that evil in her and not loving her self, her sacrificial self—even when she knows that IT is the power, not the original self in her, and she begins to see what the spirit of her unconscious dumbness is doing to both of them—even when she sees their relationship as two devils having sex and making baby devils—even then, she cannot shake free from her compulsiveness.

So the spirit that the man called up out of the woman to serve his pride now rules him body and soul. Her love was born of hate. She loves to hate, to condemn, to get revenge on unloving man, all the men who have failed her. But still this hateful judgment on all mankind is not of her own making, but is the work of her master, the devil. Ironic, isn't it, that man in his egotism actually teaches a woman how to love him to death?

If a woman hopes to break free from her destructive compulsions the first thing she must ask herself is: Do you see that your love was born of hatred? It is not an easy charge for an ego to admit to, and a woman's pride is likely to come up with all kinds of justification for her basically unloving behavior toward men, but she must not be afraid to come to grips with the possibility that she is guilty as charged.

After all, from a woman's viewpoint, there is some consolation in knowing that it all started with male sexual pressure. But she must also consider that it was a problem to the man too, and she did not have to license him to wallow in it as a means of gaining control over him and the family. The fact is that the smallest seed of hatred, like the proverbial rotten apple, ruins the entire family, no matter how respectable it may appear on the surface, and if she is to save her children, she must find her way back to innocence and real love.

3

To Serve Is to Rule

As I said in the last chapter, and as you yourself may have noticed, the world in general is run for the most part by imbeciles and dictators, bureaucrats of all kinds. Such inferior types slide easily, almost naturally, into positions of authority and power. Once firmly entrenched, they begin to eat away at the vitality of democracy while living high on the hog themselves.

How does such a state of affairs come about? Well, in the first place, we the people do not know how to stop electing corrupt politicians. Our own inherent weakness compels us to elect charlatans to take charge of our affairs. It is a weakness that has been handed down through the human race since the world began, and it is almost impossible to detect. Why? Because we are blinded to its presence by our prideful need to be recognized as the "godlings" we suppose ourselves to be. All a mediocre person has to do is to pay homage to this notion we have of ourselves by means of a little graceful groveling, building us up while putting himself down, and he is on the way to becoming our master.

Surely this topsy-turvy situation is not entirely strange to you. At one time or another, you have met that "greatest person in the world," the one you have waited for all your life. The one who makes you feel like a god. So you get married, and all hell breaks loose. She starts to take liberties, make demands, spend your money, and you can't do a damn thing about it. Or, he who once called you "his queen" now sees you as his chattel and gives you the back of his hand at the first sign of "uppityness." Behold, the servant has become the master. The one who winds up with the power is always the one who has been the most successful at playing the submissive, adoring role. The one who knows, and doesn't hesitate to live by, this time-honored principle: *To serve is to rule.*

The ability to blind a person to his ego failing with praise, and then to service his growing weakness and "save" him from guilt with false affection—this is the instrument of power for those who are sufficiently ruthless to use it. And this is the power that corrupts the corrupter absolutely.

No matter how hard a person might try to grab and hang onto the short end of the stick, to abase himself and reverse the power paradox, he can not do so. He will emerge dominant. The veriest coward is a tyrant in secret. The battered wife is typical of a woman trying to make herself small and non-threatening out of fear of becoming like the person she most resents, her mean domineering father. You might say that the ploy has backfired in her case; yet she remains the one in power, the one pushing the buttons, *his* buttons.

Having married what she thought would be a good man (a weak one, of course, because her father was violent), a woman soon discovers that her "love" is making him weaker than he was in the first place. Soon, to her horror, she sees the same violence in him as there was in the father she hated. In an effort to reverse the process and give him back his manhood (an impossible task) she starts to bully him and make outrageous demands, hoping thereby to make him mad enough to stand up to her, thinking that if and when he does, she will back down and transfer to him the honor of holding the whip hand. All too often this strategy fails. The man becomes a cowering wimp, and she becomes the father she hated. When the strategy does work, when the man does react to her manipulation with rage, she gives in to his violence and begins to revel in her martyrdom, for now she is able to judge him without having to face the violence within herself. She sees herself "suffering for righteousness' sake," the role she took refuge in as a child. And the monkey is on *his* back.

The problem with acquiring a sense of goodness by this means is that it depends entirely on making the other person wrong. By responding to the man in a fearful cowardly way she goads him to new heights of frustrated tyranny, so that she can see her own weakness as "goodness" compared to the obvious "badness" she has created in him for contrast. A woman can not stand up to a violent abusive husband for fear of becoming like the father who set her up to hate him. Nevertheless, her hatred is making her violent inside. That is why she feels compelled to submit to the bully and remain the victim in order to serve her secret need to judge. Do you see how a woman's spirit, even in a battered state, can triumph? "Impossible! How can that be?" you ask. Look again, carefully.

Once a woman has created a beast to serve her ego's need to sit in judgment, she gains control of the children. They naturally hate the beast that mother's love has created, so they turn against their father and worship their mother. She becomes the government, the power, the refuge the children seek. He is the devil they cast out. She is the good, the martyr, the god. What the children fail to see is that their mother has succeeded through "love" in creating a projection of the father who violated her. She knows instinctively that unless she projects the evil that lurks inside herself into her husband, she will be the one to emerge violent and domineering.

Often a woman will be so fearful of being dominated by her husband, as she has been by her father, that she will pick a weak man to relate to in order to retain the upper hand in their relationship even though she senses instinctively that it is not her proper role. (As they say, "It's lonely at the top," especially for a woman.) Only when she becomes disgusted with her own proclivity for violence will she seek a man who will dominate her. And there she is, the victim again, even as she was in her childhood.

Now, in order to avoid becoming like the father she hated, she is locked into remaining a victim and cultivating in her husband the very qualities that she still hates in her father; so that as his violence evolves, it will serve her with the illusion that her own "goodness" is rising to new heights. Meanwhile, this process of promoting her husband to be an object of judgment is causing her to become that which she hates. Like it or not, it happens. Do you see the dilemma? The battered woman is so terrified of discovering the awful truth about herself that she accepts the pain of abuse in order to fixate on the evil she sees in all men, and thus distract herself from seeing the evil in the role she is playing.

Some women love the power game. They covet the masculine role and enjoy attaining to a position of bullying, authoritarian rule through the process of submissiveness already described. That kind of female enjoys nagging and challenging men to back down. She is comfortable in the role of turning men into cowering wimps. She enjoys turning the tables on men and making them suffer a woman's lot in life. She turns them into some semblance of the little girl she once was while she takes on the role of the male inflicting torture. But in every case where a "man" becomes a submissive lackey and begins serving the man inside his wife, he will drive her to violence, and "he" (the "she" in him) will look like the angel. He will turn the children against the drinking, smoking, two-timing manly woman; and the womanly man then becomes the governing influence that will spoil the kids rotten.

If such a "man" were to become a politician, he would be a liberal and have us all on welfare. There is no escaping the fact that anything that serves you becomes your tyrant, be it man, woman, food, sex, dope, or alcohol. Sooner or later, you will discover that it is ruling you and is no longer your servant. So you seek another "servant," and before you know it, it has become your next tyrant.

Let us say that you find yourself a prisoner of the kind of love I have been writing about, and you react in a fit of rage in order to *force* your wife to pay you respect. You have long since discarded the romantic notions you once cherished of love and devotion, having discovered them to be totally irrelevant to the situation you find yourself in; so you try to regain the power and authority you once thought you had through sheer force and violence. But you can't win. No matter how you put her down, or no matter how much she cooperates with you by putting *herself* down by acting small, dumb, fearful, and helpless, you will end up the loser. Her cowering reactions to your strength challenge your male ego to go to greater extremes to show her just how big and strong you are; but the more you beat her down, the more you are acting out of the "beast" side of your nature, and the less of a man you are becoming. And no matter how big a beast you become, you can not completely escape your conscience. In your efforts to do so, you will become ruthlessly addicted to being served and glorified, knocking others down to build yourself up. But always, at the back of your conscience where you have shoved it, lives the nagging awareness that you are becoming less of a man with every "victory."

When the ego is helped to become prideful through being stroked, served, or serviced, *it is always lowered and degraded.* You have to be in the shoes of a beast/man to know what this is like. And chances are, if you've lived long enough, even if you are a woman, you have had some brush with it: the violence you feel toward those who kneel and cower before you, the surge of feelings of superiority, accompanied immediately by a sense of being debased, degraded, and trapped, made subject at almost the same instant. The madness of ego satisfaction's becoming instant dissatisfaction. The torment of a slave in hell drives him to degrade the degrader until, spurred on by his cowering fear of becoming just like the oppressor, he kills her for what she is covertly doing to him, or she kills him for what he is overtly doing to her.

The sad thing about all this is that it would never have happened if the woman had not fallen to hatred of her father and become addicted to "loving" weak or wicked men as a means of puffing them up into objects of hate and judgment. The same principle applies to women who abuse their children. They are as strong before the weak as they are weak before the strong. The helpless state of a little child brings out the beast (the man) in the woman who has become her husband/father in the process of hating all men.

4

Another Round in the Battle
of the Sexes

In the ongoing battle of egos, known as the battle of the sexes, the weapon most favored by women is their ability to sow confusion in the man they are trying to dominate. And it usually works. In any confrontation between the strong and the weak, all the weaker person has to do is start to whittle away at the belief system and self-confidence of her adversary. In this she must be very persistent, chipping away without let-up until she finally penetrates the armor of his integrity.

For the most part, women are totally unaware of their ability to confound and dominate men by this means; and any attempt to make them aware of what they are doing is likely to make them angry and more confusing than ever. At this point, they can be extremely dangerous. Because sowing confusion is their stock in trade, they are naturally threatened by any display of logic or any attempt to "clear the air."

Observe now how the weaker sex conquers the stronger by appearing to submit to him in every area. It is really quite easy to see how she does this if you understand a very simple rule of thumb: namely, support him when he is wrong, and if he is not wrong, upset him and make him wrong. Then, submit. Give him the support he craves. But now, the support is for the implanted wrong.

A moral man, one who is sure of himself, needs no sympathy or reassurance from his environment or anyone in it, because the ground of his being, his strength, is within himself. Unfortunately, the world is not exactly overrun with men so well centered that they are impervious to the tease of their environment and thus incapable of becoming upset.

The average man, even if he is right in principle in any given instance, can be intimidated and upset by a guileful woman. At this point, a "wrong" factor enters the picture; and the woman who goes along with the man after she has succeeded in upsetting him is lending her support to his altered state. The situation is entirely different from what it would have been had she gone along with him in the first place; that is, before she started the argument that upset him. The net effect is to weaken the man, so that he loses his independence and develops a growing need for the woman's support in future decisions.

The same simple principle works equally well with praise. For instance, a kid might make something in his father's workshop that turns out to be unusually well done. He will naturally welcome the family's acknowledgment that he did a good job. He might even welcome a few constructive suggestions for doing it even better the next time. What he respects and needs at this time is an objective opinion. Now, do I really have to tell you how the average mother reacts to her son's achievement? With extravagant praise, excitement, wild dreams of future triumphs. The poor kid hardly knows what hit him; but if he accepts this lavish praise as his due, he will henceforth be deprived of the power to do well on his own.

From that day on, he will: 1) be afraid to succeed because he simply can't handle the praise-engendered emotions that have made him fall from innocence, or 2) become completely dependent on encouragement and praise from others in all that he does. He may achieve a degree of success, but he will be filled with anxiety about it and may even give it up. The ramifications and complications of this sad state are legion.

People who put you on a pedestal secretly want to be in charge. They know instinctively that to serve a person's ego is eventually to rule it. While the seducer is in the process of stroking your ego, even though you may indeed be the head of a household and chairman of the board, that clever people-pleasing person's most convincing, patronizing personality is taking over; he knows that he is secretly in control, even now. He already feels his power and is confident that his deceitful undermining of your position of authority is working. Your very belief and trust in your flatterer transfers the power into his hands. Women and politicians serve in order to rule. You elect them to serve you, but you wind up serving them.

The doting wife who closes her eyes to her husband's faults is secretly undermining his authority over the children. He goes to work thinking all is well at home, but what is actually happening there? All too often, in too many homes, this doting wife is spoiling the kids rotten, weakening them to need her supportive "love." No matter what they do wrong, she goes along with it and smooths things over, assuring them that "daddy won't have to know." So when daddy gets home and finds that his kids are running wild and not following his instructions, he gets upset, and his wife sets about to calm him down with her "love." Thus she sets in motion the process of projecting a fault and then nurturing it in the name of love.

A truly guileful woman can do such a number on the children that they feel justified in their disobedience and may flout dad's authority quite openly, often driving him to violence. He doesn't suspect that his wife is supporting a rebellion against him. He means well. He lays down the rules as he should. But his wife sees to it that his rules don't work, that *his* love and authority will fail, and he will have to resort to violence. All the while, *her* "love" seems to work and command respect. She may even believe it is all that holds the family together! Now the same principle can apply to your most trusted employees, those who are most loyal, who can't do enough for you. They take on tremendous responsibility, and on the surface at least they seem to agree with you 100%. By now, they have won your confidence and undying respect. You don't know, of course, that this paragon of virtue hates your guts and resents your authority, your power, your money, your charisma. This type of person could never have achieved the status that you have come into naturally, so he or she will do his best to rob you of it. And you will provide such conniving employees with the means to accomplish their dirty work through the absolute trust you place in them. As they take on more and more of your role, under the guise of making things easier for you, they proceed to ruin your business. Or they steal you blind. They certainly can't run the business as you do. Their jealousy and conniving have robbed them of grace, so they can achieve only by undermining your authority with flattery and insincere support.

In the exact same way, an ambitious woman will get her hooks into an ambitious man. She will help him in his climb as long as it is in her best interest to do so. But once he has it made, she walks away with the loot and the children. Very often men, and even children, will sense what is going on in the home under the surface, and in an effort to rebel against the woman's hypocritical support, will fail on purpose. They come to fear any success they might achieve through such a woman. Sensing the danger, but not knowing exactly how to cope with it openly, they begin to think that the only way they can know success is by defeating *her* success, *her* ride to glory and power on *their* dumb backs.

Most often, the domestic squabbles over money, success, or laziness, arise from a woman's being stuck with the kind of man who is waging the kind of rebellion we have been discussing. And, boy, is she mad! Serves her right. Her will is totally frustrated. She can't make it on her own, without a man (a donkey) to go out and get what she motivates him to get, so she has to seduce her way to power.

Beware the seducer, be it male or female. Watch out for the person who always agrees with you. Watch out also for the one who can't stand your being right and gives you a hard time until he manages to upset you, at which point he suddenly goes along with you, knowing that you have fallen from grace in the heat of battle. The power of this type of person rests entirely on serving an existing fault, or on creating one, mostly through intimidation, and then seeking to soothe it.

5

The Altered Man: Prisoner of Trauma

What a selfish man's weakness draws to him, and what, in his deluded mind, he sees as loving and being loved, sucks him to death. Man is born in sin, and sin is trauma, a failing of every father, transmitted through every mother since Eve.

The spirit of trauma (sin) is a dictator. It dictates what you eat and drink, who will be your mate, the good and evil in your life, how you think and feel about anything. And you can be sure that every "choice" will be dead wrong and will draw you through a series of spiraling tragedies ever closer to hell. The spirit of trauma blinds you to reality and never allows you to see the face of truth.

We are all prisoners of trauma, and even though we may come to know the difference between right and wrong, through guilt, and try to resist wrongdoing, we really cannot do so with our whole being. Resolutions fail. Lust is master. Our souls lust after the wrong.

The natural man, born of trauma, cannot long exist apart from the trauma that created him. The spirit of trauma within us cannot tolerate peace; it is therefore bound to create the intrigue it needs to grow from. The altered man can no longer act out of natural motivation, even when he understands what is natural. We need tease and cruel pressure in order to grow. Pride, evolving from the sin of trauma, cannot survive apart from a trauma source; so the alien self within you draws you to intrigue and problems for the sake of its own evolution. That is why you are afraid to give up the "life" of sin, for sin is the life of the fallen self, and this self goes on to seek out its trauma source for its completion.

Sin (false love or naked hate) creates hunger, and hunger, once serviced and gratified by the trauma source, is the fulfillment of pride. The pleasure of this fulfillment is the only happiness an earthbound man can know.

Creating needs through tease, then servicing them, re-creates the sinful need over and over again, and begets an endless hunger, an infernal "love" affair. Since trauma is both an escape and a denial of reality, man sees only *love* where betrayal lurks. The love of food and sex betrays him and breeds the sin, or trauma, of hate and love/hate. They are the life of pride, but it is a life that leads to spiritual and physical decay.

If men are to survive the hell they have created for themselves through their use of women, they must come to realize that the greater part of their sex drive is not natural. For the most part, a man's lust has been awakened by a need for ego reassurance, and that need rises from a trauma/sin source, a role that they insist on the woman's filling for them.

Man's thought of woman itself represents a rejection of God, and makes woman, in a glance, the reinforcing power of his trauma/sin. The inclination of his soul is toward the woman and draws her image to mind, causing him to force her into an unnatural role in which his ambitious soul can find solace. The trauma/sin of rejecting God to *be* God has its origin in the mind, or imagination. Sin is kept eternally alive through being called to mind in fantasy.

Male sexuality is the gross symptom of a failing need—a spiritual weakness—a need to be loved (glorified) for that very failing. For example, if you resent someone, that is a sin, the sin of unforgiveness, judgment. Every time you think of that person, recalling your hurt compulsively to mind over and over again, you become still more resentful and judgmental. The sin of sustained hate leads to more judgment, more pride, more sin, more sexual awakening. And the guilt of judgment is amplified, kept alive as pride, through resentment, even though the person you resent is no longer a part of your environment and may even be dead.

It is in this way that a man's ego becomes painfully addicted to hating, in order to keep his judgmental self-righteousness alive. The pride of man keeps him "loving," dreaming, and drooling over food and sex. Whoever holds a love/hate thought in his mind has already committed and reinforced the sin of pride that has caused his fall into sensuality.

The movement away from God, rejection, leads to an involvement with images. The man whose pride is being stroked, and apparently served, by the spirit of images, is actually a slave to the spirit of illusion. Just thinking about a traumatic-romantic event acts on the consciousness in such a way as to make it happen all over again. The sensual arousal, the devolution of dark yearning, results from the simple act of "taking to thought." Taking to thought happens to be a "choice," a rejection of truth in order to continue on pride's way.

You might recall my saying that rejection of God is the basis of sin. That rejection leads to the fall as it causes pathological and psychological alterations of man's being and imprints him with a compulsive mindfulness of his new allegiance, a yearning to be complete with it. His reaction of lust in the name of love, and his hateful judgments as the prerogative of pride, harden him in his rejection of the Creator. He loses his soul in extreme emotions and the self-righteous dreaming that saves him from facing reality. His pride finds salvation in emotion.

Just as a flag symbolizes everything a country stands for, so does the female image, when recalled to mind, symbolize the power of the original doubt, the chink in the armor of faith that led us to a wrong kind of faith through emotion and reinforced our reliance on the proud egotistical way. Beware the pull of emotion, all emotion, the emotion of love, as well as the emotion of hate.

The process of pridefully dreaming away reality awakens sensual body hungers that we feed with seductive images in order to enhance their power over us and to reinforce our bondage to sensuality; but no matter how deeply we sink into the spirit of ambition and pride, we will never outrun our guilt, even though we may be half-consciously using it to put an edge on our carnal delights.

Has your capacity for objective awareness ever caught you in that split second of surrender to your dark side, that momentary blink of an eyelid, when your stubborn soul called upon emotional imaginings to save you from truth and from guilt? Have you noted that moment of "deliverance," when you escaped to fulfill an ancient promise, along with its ancient curse? The image reassures, the soul believes the lie and sinks thankfully into the dream; and as it does, evil displaces good, sexual desire is quickened, and your world dissolves into the rapture of acceptance—relief from the guilt of sin, the tension of hunger.

We seem to be caught in a never-ending cycle. An unnatural tension—sex drive, or lust—is awakened by the false resolve of man's soul to be his own god, and as he feeds the sexual tension with his imagination, his soul is accepted for its selfishness, and he loses himself in sin once again. But we never outrun our guilt. The cycle continues, anxiety builds, and we continue to seek refuge in our dreams.

Men have fallen low; they have become gross, prideful animals. And because they are proud, they never can admit their wrong. The nature of the proud one is to reject truth, and to seek emotional recognition by means of the very emotions that led to his downfall.

Men take pleasure in their degradation, because it acts as a challenge to their pride—the baser the desire, the prouder they must grow in their defense of it. But guilt trails pride as surely as night follows day. So men dream of food and women continuously. They dare not allow a space, a pause, a moment of quiet, lest the world of their illusion, in which they reign supreme as King Ego, disintegrate and leave them naked in the Light of Reality.

The die is cast—the choice has been made. Man's soul must wallow like a pig in forbidden, ever grosser thoughts and hungers, until the sheer pain of it, the debilitation and ravaging of his whole being, stops him cold, as it usually does with disease or death, or drives him to seek refuge on higher ground.

Understand that hunger, lust, gluttony—when gratified and glorified—lead to abject slavery. The understanding and sympathetic person who accepts you in spite of your bondage to these weaknesses—who loves your gross psychotic devotions, and dedicates himself to keeping you emotionally secure and happy in your selfish pleasures and delusions of grandeur—is your betrayer and destroyer. He (usually, she) is hell's usher.

Hell's female usher has usually been driven to play this supporting role by the guilt she feels over having responded to male pressure. Sexual pressure (the cry for help of a wounded ego) is the force that upsets her and persuades her to give up her chastity. So, the guilt of her trauma (her sin of resenting, and then giving in to, pressure) causes her to see man as the superior beast, worthy of the dedicated service and worship that constitute her own claim to glory.

She, too, has a dream. She escapes into images. She becomes sexually addicted to male lust as a substitute for the true love she lost through having yielded herself to a man. Her support makes men grub and grunt for her; and when she loses herself in the effect she has on a man, the ecstasy of her fallen self resembles that of a vampire more than the ecstasy of a real person. How sad it is to think that this is the only love known to men and women.

A woman's hatred toward men's use of her, her hatred of men for dredging up the worst in her to serve the worst in them—this is what turns her true love and respect into a perverted love for the worst in man, in exchange for his giving the worst in himself, his only life, to her, along with the worship that makes her his god. A woman dreams of finding love in a man by giving him what he wants, only to wind up on a pedestal, possessed of a power for which she has no constructive use.

In the beginning, a woman never foresees that her dreams will be realized only at the expense of a man's dying to her growing compulsion to absorb him, simply by using the power he has placed in her hands. She may not really want to—but there it is, like an itch begging to be scratched. She persists in her dream of finding real love with such a longing that she fails to see what an evil, selfish, destructive love she has fallen into.

And so it is that man in his way, and woman in her way, evolve hell's love between them. They live in a dream world together until the pain forces them either to wake up, or die to truth (the option most frequently taken). Loving and blaming each other, they die; for the wages of sin is death, and sin is the evolution of pride through forbidden love.

The female hatred of men for their use of women is not a comfortable emotion for a woman to bear; so, to assuage her guilt, she dreams of finding redemption through sharing the man's enthusiasm for lust. She thus sets herself up to play the corrupt role demanded of her by the man who dreams about women as the result of having been violated by one. The dream love, made real, becomes liar and violator. Every violated woman needs a weak man to violate with lying love; she must absorb his life to make her dream of love and security come true. Her ego needs a failing man to live through. Without a failing man, a falling woman can not continue to dream, and to will her way to the tragedy of happiness. She must wake up. But where, oh where, can Sleeping Beauty ever find a noble man to kiss her with real love and rescue her from the hell of her dreams?

Learn, then, to let resentment pass, and when you have overcome resentment, poise, balance, and true love will enter—or reenter—your life. To the degree you let resentment toward intimidation pass, to that degree will your need for false love diminish, for forgiveness is rewarded by God's love. You will feel less need for earthly loves and delights. You will stop being a people pleaser, a frustrated slave of pleasure.

Your joy in triumphing over temptation will far outweigh the pleasure you once found in yielding to it. You will know a joy without end, without limit: the joy of eating without being eaten, having without being had, possessing without being possessed. You will find in self-denial the love you could never find in selfishness.

6

The Spirit of the Lie

The mystical excitement that is the life of the male ego, and is aroused by the female presence, differs markedly from the excitement that is aroused in the female by the male presence. Men are subject to the female presence from birth, whereas women are subject to the male presence *for* their presence. Simply, v*is-à-vis* male-female relationships, women feel what they can make men feel.

When a woman feels sexually receptive, it is as the result of her "success" with the male. So, if a woman can arouse an artificial need within herself, her ego can experience the animal life of it. She arouses that need by stroking a male ego and participating in the effect it has on him. In a sense, then, the "life" of a vain woman becomes dependent on arousing a man's feeling for her. Her need for *him* is parasitic on *his* need for *her;* so her destiny will be shaped by her compulsion to tempt or nag the life out of a man in order to make him fall for her.

From the man's viewpoint, women are love/hate objects. He hates the woman who betrays his love by using him instead of loving him back; but his hatred provides his nagging wife with still another temptation, another reaction for her ego to feed on. And when he finds himself "shut out," his male need for her approval will grow stronger than ever. Try as he might, a man will always fail in his attempt to use hate as a defense against love's bondage. Instead of saving him from the tyranny of love, it increases his fixation to the woman, and eventually, the guilt of hating will cause him to cry out to her for love.

From the cradle, all male egos are fascinated by images of woman. They seduce him from the divine love and become the source of his re-creation. Sin, or trauma, enters his life as the result of his displacement from one source of creation and love to another, from God's will to the female will. Through his attachment to her, he begins to enter a new order of existence on earth—as it is in hell.

The emotions of love and hate are not opposites; both are responses to temptation, and both swell the male ego. The temptation of love leads to the betrayal by love, and betrayal leads to hate and blame. Hate is the lower level of temptation, more deadly than love, but certain to lead back to the need for love.

One can often derive as much ego satisfaction and fulfillment from feelings of rejection and hate as from the feeling of love. Both are forms of obedience to hell. (Of course, I'm speaking here of "love" as the "feeling" with which we usually equate it, inasmuch as divine love is not a feeling or an emotion in any sense of the word.) Resentment produces judgment, and judgment swells pride until it becomes addicted to being hurt and rejected for its growth. Resentment, then, renews and revitalizes pride, just as false love does. Hating a person for his wickedness can be just as revitalizing to our pride as being loved.

We lavish all our attention on the love/hate intrigue that revolves around evil, and it thrives on that attention, for by wallowing in it to the exclusion of all else, we cut ourselves off from any awareness of what God might have had in mind for us. When we respond with "love" or "hate," we join forces with the spirit of our downfall; surrendering to sin, we reinforce its authority and control over our lives.

The confirmed sinner has no recourse—he must continue to sin in order to justify and complete the imperfect self that has accepted the spirit of evil as its master. Sin is exciting and magnetic because it offers fulfillment to the self that we identify, mistakenly, as "us." Who among us can not remember flying into a towering rage over some slight or insult to his ego, real or imagined? Once hate gets a firm grip on us, we milk it for all the emotional value it can give us, searching our memory bank frantically for evidence of past trespasses against us on the part of our oppressor, adding fuel to the fire of our rage with all the pent-up energy at our command, lest it die away and leave us empty and forsaken on the field of devastation—as it always does.

Those of us who have managed to mature to some extent, whether or not we have found complete salvation from our emotions, have at least learned to be wary of them enough to hang onto a measure of control over them; so we might have to look back to the temper tantrums of our childhood in order to recall the "highs" of hate. Not so, perhaps, when we look at the highs of infatuation. Both emotions, love and hate, seem to offer us so much, but when the storm has passed, we find that we have paid for our rage, or our ecstasy, with our lives—all the identity we have left is an empty shell, crying out to be filled. (The readers who happen to have arrived at this stage of need are the ones most likely to change direction and go the distance with me, because there is something about our stubborn egos that keeps us tied to the same wrong ways until we hit bottom.)

I have belabored the love/hate connection in order to make you men aware of why you are attracted to women who possess the very qualities you most hated in your mother. Your hatred of women started with your hatred of the unloved, guileful, or downright wicked woman who happened to be your mother, and it set you up to be excited by, and attracted to, her kind of woman. When you set out in search of a wife, it is your mother, whether you think you loved her or know you hated her, whose nature will serve as your criterion in the selection process. She will govern your choice, like it or not. You can't fight destiny.

To overcome the woman inside him, to establish himself as the man-child of God, a man must overcome the woman outside him. He must love the hell *out* of her, not *in* her. He must call forth the woman out of the female by denying himself the love he craves of her. He cannot stand as a source of love for his wife until the love that he bears her has been purged of his need for her.

But if a man hates a woman for the troubles that have arisen as the result of his own failing with her, his guilt before God grows more intense—as does his need for the woman's love to help him to hide and deny that guilt.

Sin begins as an idea that enters through the forbidden zone of imagination to tear us away from Paradise, that objective state of mind in which we are subject only to God's bidding. Sin fires up our imagination with the idea that we can be whatever we want to be, and do whatever we want to do—turn abstractions into tangible realities and create our own heaven on earth. But man must not aspire to be his own God. If one man can be a god, then all men can be gods. And where is the overshadowing Principle, the Unifying Force to bring order to such an arrangement?

When man aspires to be his own God, he opens the door to evil, and evil establishes itself at the very core of his being, where it strives to work its will on earth as it does in hell. Man falls into his mind and loses contact with the bright consciousness that was his birthright.

Strangely enough, when a man loses his original consciousness, thanks to the invasion of evil, he feels that he is actually waking up, like Alice in Wonderland. The trauma of the forbidden has so transformed him that his dreams look real and possible of fulfillment. The spirit that has taken him over fills him with a false hope, and a new faith in the new master. He feels that he is off to a fresh start—as indeed he is, now that his point of reference has turned 180 degrees; for now, with the wrong spirit in charge of his consciousness, all that is evil looks right and good to him, whereas all that is good troubles his new and perverted "conscience."

Emotional "highs" are ego trips, a kind of trauma, and all trauma leads to that fallen state of consciousness wherein we identify the voice of the serpent as our own will, and the love we crave is the lie that reinforces our false purpose and agrees with our false conscience. This kind of love leads naturally to the next traumas: hate and blame, otherwise known as resentment and judgment. Then, of course, the guilt of resentment drives us back to the hate object (the former love object) for more of the crippling love. We think that our guilt feelings have been caused by our having sinned against the love/hate object, but it is our true conscience we sin against when we fall to *any* prideful emotion.

Men use love to deny reality and to escape from guilt, but a love so motivated leads inevitably to betrayal—back to its starting point, actually, for that kind of love is a betrayal of Divine Love.

Over and over again, "love" robs man of the opportunity to repent of his sinful ways and change his course. Following its lure, he is constantly falling into the pit of despair. False love, for the false man, always "saves" and betrays, and both the love trauma and the hate trauma feed on the nature that was altered by the original trauma. Often, we hate people for praising us in our imperfect state, and we become cruel to them in an attempt to stop them from destroying the last vestiges of true hope that remain in our consciousness. Alas, they react by thinking they have failed to love us enough, so they shower more love on us, partly in an effort to escape their resentment of our rejection.

All egos need trauma in order to grow, to escape, to be free from Truth in order to evolve along their own selfish, egocentric plan. All egos go to extremes in everything, from love to hate, from too much sex to no sex at all, from overeating to starvation diets—even to suicide, not living at all, the ego's antidote to living improperly.

We are trauma-based beings; we need intrigue in order to exist. We look for trouble. We cannot exist without a center of evil to love/hate. Everything you think you love you also secretly hate. Any absolute loyalty, to cigarettes, wife—that special closeness to mother—is simply a deeper than average commitment to a lie. It must lead, eventually, to some awareness of your plight; but when it does, you try to put out that awareness by losing yourself in the excitement of other loves and hates. As long as you are ruled by pride, you cannot free yourself of debilitating influences. Your ego needs them in order to escape God's way, as it is known to you through your original intuition and consciousness, and to escape into the evolution of "self." You need your poisons to help you believe in your way, to help you live the faith of doubt, the faith in the lie.

"I can stop smoking if I want to," you say, "but I choose to smoke." You use this face-saving pronouncement when you refuse to face up to the obvious truth about your attachments. You make slavery appear to be your very own choice, your act of willing devotion. Your "love" for anything merely means that you want it, when, as a matter of fact, it has made you want it, and has convinced you that *its* way is *your* way. Like God, "it" creates desires for itself in you, so that you will fulfill its purpose of hell on earth through your surrender to its will.

When you react to the external temptation of evil excitement, it changes your nature. Henceforth, you will seek to fulfill its spirit through every forbidden pleasure. You cannot escape its "love," and its stroking of your ego will convince you that you are growing, but it is the evil spirit that is growing strong in you behind the camouflage of "love." The change that has been wrought in your inner self causes you to gravitate toward external conditions that echo the one that first implanted itself in you and made you hunger for evil. Yet you carry on under the illusion that you are good.

All emotions are wolves in sheeps' clothing, and when you put a woman on a pedestal, worshiping her like a god, you are promoting her to become a devil in disguise. While your introduction to false love was through a woman, the hypnosis of that first encounter has spread to encompass everything associated with it: persons, places, weather, the time of day—all the heady, romantic stuff of nostalgia.

So if the "right" person comes along at the "right" time in the "right" place, he appears to you to be bathed in the glamorous aura of the seductive spirit that has taken you over, and you will follow him anywhere. (Or her, as the case may be.) If it happens to be a drug pusher, you will become hypnotically fixated to him and his drugs, and he will push you around the rest of your life. You will be his victim, but it will be *your* need, *your* craving that will provide your manipulator with the power to require almost anything of you in return for supplying you with the wherewithal to satisfy your craven need. With each fulfillment, you fall a little deeper into the pit, and your need to be corrupted (loved) in order to feel served and "saved" will burn more intensely than before. Each appeasement of such a hunger creates a greater hunger.

Now you can understand why fans of the Olympic Games were willing to stand in such long lines after the Games were over in order to purchase all kinds of mementos: freeway signs, buttons, banners—anything to delay their descent from the empyrean cloud of excitement and triumph into the real world. That not-so-innocent "innocent" excitement had subtly traumatized them and addicted them to a need for memorabilia in order to hang onto the Olympic spirit. The mementos act as drugs by posthypnotically reactivating the exciting spirit of the games. Once an object becomes associated with the original trauma, it takes on the ability to act in its place. A distinctive perfume will bring to mind the person you know who wears it, along with the emotions her physical presence would evoke in you.

Any object you associate with the original ego excitement, or trauma, will perpetuate in you the effect of that first experience. A commemorative plaque, a seductive poster, a prayer cloth, a song—all reinforce the power of the original sin and keep alive in you the illusions of power and glory to which you have become addicted. Indulgence in sentimentality is dangerously addictive. It acts as an iron curtain between the never-never land of illusion and your true self. For God's sake, to say nothing of your own, tear it down. Get rid of it.

You might ask, "How?" How *does* one rid himself of the food he has to eat in order to stay alive? Before I get to the answer, let's ponder a moment on how quickly our need to survive, physically and spiritually, boils down to the natural act of eating. Was it not consummately shrewd of the serpent to inject his will into us through food? Some of our nutritionists go so far as to say that we *are* what we eat, and to a great extent, they are right. We are transformed and shaped by what we take into our bodies; but we are equally transformed and traumatized by our emotional attachments. All attachments and appeals to our senses are variations of the same old theme of temptation. Where is the ego that won't bite on the opportunity to seize the godhead for himself? But don't you see that when he does, his ego is thenceforth manipulated and enslaved by the corrupting spirit behind the sinful offering? It is written: *The love of the world makes you God's enemy.*

As soon as you fall for any ego-appealing object or desire, you become traumatized. A trauma self takes up residence within you, and you become fixated to the time, place, form, sound, color—everything you associate with the magical essence of the transforming agent. You become imprinted with the memory of your new birth, and you must gravitate toward it compulsively, like a crazed homing salmon. You crave constant renewal from the source of your creation.

When tempted, we respond, first, with feelings of attraction—later, perhaps, with revulsion. First, we love, and then we run in hate and horror from the love object, only to embrace another "love" object. Then, love betrays us again. Finally, done in by "love," we become afraid of the love we need. We retreat into daydreams, and they metamorphose into nightmares. We are matadors who conquer bulls only in our imagination, and whatever glory we find there is just more of the same delusion. We never overcome evil, for we are constantly falling to deception, and hell is still pulling our strings through our fantasies. All sin begins when we fall into our minds in our effort to seek refuge from God, our Creator; and as long as we live in our minds, sin lives on through us.

Any lingering consciousness of guilt compels our pride to sanctify and attach itself to increasingly depraved ideas and acts. The lower we sink, the more we find evil exciting, the closer we come to the origin, the mystery, of our re-creation, the original spirit of corruption.

Loves, as "saviors," are betrayers. They pull you into a hellish "heaven," peopled with hell's angels and their forbidden delights, beckoning you toward their mock paradise through the lowest, filthiest rituals imaginable. So you run from one bed or one job to another, one downward "transcendental" experience to another, always seeking an escape from conscience for the sake of some selfish ego fulfillment, becoming more debilitated by each new adventure, each new attachment, each new "love."

Everything you do is self-defeating. You give your money, your life, your labor; you trade your body and soul for the approval of some fallen soul. But for the prideful, there is no escape from the hell of love and hate. All wrong people need worldly lying love.

All our experiences draw us back to the cradle of our original trauma. Men return to their mothers in their wives; women return to their mothers in their weak husbands. At this point, we teeter on the brink of decision: We may elect to understand and unravel the mystery by yielding to its awakening pain and struggling toward the light, or we can simply wallow in whatever excitement value it provides, and let it run its dreary course. Take your choice.

Stop seeking sensual love. After all, what are the fleshly delights of food and love, anyway, other than the proud trumpeting of the spirit of your rebellion? Depose that lying tyrant and prepare for the journey to the Light.

Love, as most of us experience it, and hate are both forms of suffering, and suffering is the life of hell. The sinner's entire life is based on tragedy. Relive for a moment the dark ages of your sinful rebellion, assuming that by now you are on the godly path—or let me rub your nose in the mess you are making of your life if you have not yet broken free. Take off the blinkers. Let's take a good look at how it is with you.

You cling to suffering, finding it somehow ennobling. You wallow in the ecstasy and agony of the love that leads to hate and back to love in a never-ending cycle. You can never know peace; you hunger for treachery and turmoil. You are unworthy of the good life, and you have convinced yourself that it would be too bland and dull for you, anyway. The only experiences you are receptive to are the "rewards" of hell, and they are all you "need" or deserve.

You will leave your good wife or your good husband and your good life to seek out the bad. The bad one makes you feel good, and the good one makes you feel bad. Even as you grow older and become less able to cavort in the sinful playgrounds, you cling to your mementos and lustful reminiscences. Now that there is so little to hope for in the future, you turn more and more from the present truths in order to regale yourself with the evocation of nostalgic scenes from the past.

Back you go, down into the bottomless pit of imagination where it all began, regressing further and further into childhood memories, all the way back to your mother. Beyond her, the spirit of hell lies in wait.

7

How to Break Free from Your Problems

There is a way of living, of having one's being, that does not depend on outside pressure to motivate and direct it. It is a way of life that springs from a source within you as the direct result of a proper relationship with God.

The life energy that wells up in you through this relationship does not come wrapped in words or feelings; rather, it rises naturally and effortlessly out of a deep understanding, a state of readiness to recognize and accept the guidance of Truth in every moment. In short, it is the meditative state of consciousness.

Why can't we seem to hang on to this blessed state of consciousness? You surely know the answer: it is the pride we inherited from Adam as the result of his choice to be his own God, apart from his Creator. This genetic inheritance of willfulness, selfishness, and pride is a handicap in itself, but when these failings are glorified and promoted by the culture we are born into, it's no wonder that we soon lose our connection to the true source of eternal life and energy and transfer our allegiance to the seductive spirit of the world that has claimed us.

Fortunately, the link to our Creator that manifests in us as conscience is not easy to extirpate and destroy completely; but unfortunately, most, if not all, of us have been seduced into doubting the truth of what it is saying. Therefore, one of the first steps we must take in order to return to a proper relationship with God is to stop doubting what our conscience is telling us. We must put it back in the driver's seat and live our lives in a way that bears witness to its presence.

Often, the upright way in which we conduct ourselves is enough to shame the people around us into waking up the conscience they have managed to put to sleep; but in the hard-shelled cases, when our example is either ignored or despised, we must be ready to extend to them the kindness of pointing out where they are going wrong. We must be sure, however, that our only object is to help them back to their true estate. If we harbor the slightest resentment or feel ourselves puffing up in judgment, we must hold our tongue and get back to the drawing board ourselves.

Whether you seek correction for yourself or for another, you must understand what went wrong by the clear light of Truth; otherwise, the disparity between the wrong that was and the right that should have been will not reveal itself clearly enough to rouse your sleeping conscience. Until our prideful way is challenged by the irrefutably right way so clearly, objectively, and unemotionally that we can no longer duck it, we cannot be shamed into repentance, and we must surely repent before we can hope to be saved. As long as you indulge your ego's craving to be stroked, you might as well give up hope for any meaningful change in your life. You may be the type of person who has to hit bottom before he can gather the strength to sit up and take a good objective look at the ego failings that he has been protecting and justifying as "just the way I am"! If so, you will just have to solicit the help of your true self, the self that has been drawn to these words in its search for relief, and realize that *there is nothing in this world, not a soul living, who can give you the answers you are seeking.* The motivation to act in a right way and to understand Truth springs from the universal consciousness we all share. I can not "lay" it on you, and you can not pull it out of me, because you already share it, and it testifies to the truth of these words. Each time you act in accordance with its direction, you strengthen your commitment to the right way and weaken the bonds that have enslaved you to the world.

First, you must see the nature of your failing, and you must see it for yourself; otherwise, you will compound your problems. If you look to a teacher, psychiatrist, or minister for direction and understanding, you will simply be taking on another God. You will increase your dependence on mere mortals, thus adding another unholy relationship to the chain of those that have already ensnared you.

Is it not a fact that all your problems have grown out of the way you have related to the people around you through your thoughts and feelings? And that you have not always been comfortable with those reactions? Most of us have accumulated a vast inventory of stock answers and expressions to help us glide effortlessly through the human shoals on the sea of our daily life. How surprised we are when someone takes our "how are you?" literally and launches into an account of his recent ups and downs. We may even wish that we had seen him first and crossed the street!

Most of us repress our thoughts and feelings simply because we don't know how to deal with them. If we open up to anyone at all, it is usually not until we have "had it up to here," and feel the need of some sympathetic stroking.

Where did we go wrong? How can we get back to living life effortlessly, in the childlike way that we know intuitively to be the right way? It may not come easy to start living life consciously, in a completely aware state from one moment to the next. After all, we have spent our lives running from our sins, anxieties, guilts, and fears. What is it that started us on our downhill course, our retreat from Reality? Until we see where we went wrong, how can we hope to start living in the Light?

Well, the first thing we must see is that our first failing, the underlying cause of all our problems, is *pride*, or *willfullness*. Pride, or any failing spawned by Pride, accounts for all the sickness, suffering, and tragedy in the world; but Pride, being what it is: the lord and master we chose over our Creator, causes us to resent seeing our faults for what they are by the bright light of Truth.

Fortunately, most of us are uneasy servants of Pride, for we retain enough sense to be ashamed when our prideful ways are exposed to the light. Nevertheless, unless we are yearning in the right direction, we will resent the shame that has made us aware of our fault, even though we know that we should "lean into" that shame, much as a person with an abscessed tooth leans into the dentist's drill, in order to break through to the joyful sadness of repentance. When you back away from your shame and choose pride over the pain of awareness, you are saying "no" to the conscience that should control your every moment.

If you are willing to realize how much resentment you have built up against being made aware, your spirit will soften enough to make you more receptive to God's will. Then, something marvelous will occur—not through any act of will or struggle on your part, but as the direct result of your having made the Truth welcome in your heart. The knowledge of Truth that enters in this way is an intelligent, revitalizing, and healing force, a complete package of knowing with a built-in motivation factor. No amount of study or effort on your part can gain it for you. It is what we know as "understanding," and all we have to do to get it is to want God's will to be done in our lives, regardless of the cost in terms of the ego-serving emotions of resentment, judgment, and addiction to lesser gods.

When you struggle with your problems, you are unconsciously rejecting truth—probably because you resent the problems that appear to be challenging your pride. See how we keep coming back to Pride? How it uses resentment to sustain itself? How it evolves to become the whole and sufficient reason for being of the fallen self? The finger of Pride is always on the trigger, ready to do battle with anything that challenges its hell-given authority. When Pride sounds the call to arms, you rise up to defend it, and by doing so, you feel justified and righteous, absolved from any guilt in the creation of your problems.

Resentment is the ploy you use to escape awareness and responsibility for your sins. As long as you can turn your attention to the other fellow's insult to your almighty pride, your own sin ceases to exist. It's as though it never existed. As Mehitabel, the cat, answered Archy, the cockroach, when he inquired as to the health of the kittens that, by her own admission some days previously, were beginning to be such a drag on her that she was ready to do violence to them: "*what* kittens?" (*archy and mehitabel,* by don marquis.)

By reaching for the sweetmeats and absolutions of Pride in order to "feel better," you are unconsciously evolving a bigger ego to give you a bigger guilt and a bigger problem with which to challenge your cowardly escape mechanisms. By going this way, you certainly are not improving your character, nor are you gaining any power over the basic problem. On the contrary, you are starving the real *you* and giving power to the evolving problem-challenged self that struggles to escape the indwelling Light.

In your pride, when challenged, you are an angry, self-righteous, omnipotent force, alone in the world with your problem. Nothing else exists for you. So you alone must pick up the gauntlet of challenge to enjoy the exhilaration of defending your "godlike" identity and evolving more pride and more ammunition with which to defend it. As a proud, dyed-in-the-wool egotist, you get a kick out of the problems that complicate your life—you need them for a sense of accomplishment and escape. They keep your ego tuned up and animated with a sense of growing and accomplishing. As you lose yourself in a complete involvement with challenge, you evolve a bigger ego, along with a prouder "creature" self. Your foolish reactions and choices challenge the proud egos in your environment to strike back and feed you with still more food for your growing sense of proud invincibility.

Under the circumstances, you cannot hope to get better in a real sense because you are completely preoccupied with the one problem you have set for yourself: the evolution of a separate godlike identity for yourself apart from God. And of course, to bring it about, you must live in a constant state of readiness to "do battle" with every challenge to your pride.

The wrong you are cosseting *inside* needs a greater wrong *outside* on which to hone its skills. No challenge=no adventure. No adventure=no growth. Of course, every problem you "solve" in a wrong way creates a bigger problem in need of a bigger solution. You may not realize you are doing it, but you are solving your problems in the same way big governments solve their problems, by creating bigger problems to cry out for bigger solutions.

Even in an occasional moment of lucidity, when you allow yourself to catch a glimpse of Truth, you are likely to intellectualize what you see and take unearned credit for it, seeing it as proof of your greatness. The deception excites you with false confidence and motivates you to roll up your sleeves and work your will on the environment as you draw energy from the challenge to change things and do things *your* way.

Another mistake you are likely to make, especially if you pride yourself on your intellect, is to commit to memory the things you should be content to simply recognize and know to be true. Memorizing locks you pridefully into an electro-chemical dimension of thought that puffs up your pride and adds to your conflicts. You think you know only because you think, because you feel, and because you are distracted from realizing what really is. When you try to use thinking as the means of knowing yourself, you reject or lose sight of the dimension of understanding, and your rash actions lead to internal conflict later, when your conscience catches up with you. Without divine direction, you use problems as a means of evolving your intellect along with your pride. Are you aware of the fine line between understanding and just plain thinking? A parrot knows how to talk, but it has no soul to observe thinking. It does not know that it knows, and it can not possibly understand what it knows. In much the same way, as long as your ego identifies with your thinking, feeling self and is ambitiously determined to remember itself as God, you will be emotionally involved in fighting problems, and all you will acquire in the vast storehouse of your learning is more pride.

Watch your intent. If your intent is pure; that is to say, if you really want to discover God's purpose in giving you life in this time and place, and if you really want to know where you went wrong so that you might get back into harmony with that purpose, that pure intent will render you totally unreceptive to imperfect knowledge and mealy-mouthed explanations that are nothing more than ego-stroking evasions. Realization will dawn in your consciousness like the rising sun and will illumine your path; and from the moment you begin to live by its light, you will find that you are no longer able to learn, or to arrive at decisions, or to be motivated in the old conventional ways. You will no longer take part in the prideful struggle to "get ahead" or to "make something of yourself." Your old selfish goals will cease to be your prime motivators—you will reexamine them by the light of your new understanding.

The way of understanding is completely other than, and cannot be reconciled with, the way of the intellect. You do not have to defend or explain it to those who are already on the path with you, and for the others explanations are completely impossible. Remember that they lack the eyes to see and the ears to hear, and save your energy for the living of the good life that will speak louder than words.

As you begin to understand, you will realize in a wordless way that right living is effortless, and you will lose your old need to struggle; and by the light of your new understanding, you will see the futility of trying to gain power by the sheer force of will. No matter how disturbing, embarrassing, or complicated the problem that confronts you appears to be, you will be able to let go of the need to react to it emotionally or intellectually. You will remain free to apply yourself to its solution. Note how living by the light of understanding relieves you of your old stumbling blocks: resentment of the challenge, and of the weakness in yourself that opened the door to it. You are no longer living life by the same old prideful terms, so you are no longer capable of reacting with the same old prideful emotions.

If, Heaven forbid, you are still wrestling with challenge as a means of escaping reality, you are rejecting God, and that is the last thing you should be wanting to do. If you have any goal at all, it should be to remain so centered, on such an even keel, that you can move this way or that in accordance with the dictates of reason in each moment. You must not allow yourself to be overcome by any excitement, pleasant or unpleasant. When challenged, choose to wait for the understanding that is greater than your own to light your path and show you the error of your ways. Let it humble you, lest pride regain its grip on you and confound you with resentment of the problem and of the Light that was showing you a better way to go.

If you are an alcoholic, you must be willing to take a good look at the way you are, and admit to what you see. Hold still, and take a good look at your resentment of the persons or conditions that you blame for having driven you to the bottle. Forget about its targets for a minute, and look at the resentment itself—how you wallow in it and comfort yourself with all the "might-have-beens" and "if-only's." See how you blame others, especially your parents, for all your shortcomings. See how your resentment is sustaining your pride in its judgment of others, while it is slowly and stealthily sentencing your body to a shameful death. See it for what it is. Then, let go of it.

You must allow old memories and anxieties to come to the surface of your consciousness while resisting the temptation to become upset by them, to push them back into the subconscious, to struggle with them or excuse them or worry about them or "gussy" them up a little to make them a bit more presentable. You must see them as they are, in all their ugliness, before you can take back the power you have given them to ruin your life. When you fully realize the futility of struggle, you will find it easier to resist the temptation to do so. You have continued to struggle with your demons only because you have been unwilling to face the pointlessness and powerlessness of your own will. Now, even if I have convinced you of the truth of what I am telling you, and you accept it on the intellectual level only, you will lack the understanding to implement what you have learned in your real-life experience. It's like "trying" to relax; trying makes you more aware of the tension.

While there is little you can do to control an involuntary reaction, like jumping when a firecracker goes off near you, you do have a measure of control over the more voluntary, or conscious, reactions—such as resentment of the person who scared you with the firecracker, or resentment of yourself for having been so off-balance that you gave him the satisfaction of seeing you jump. (Note how even the most unregenerate person is always dimly aware of the moral superiority of poise, non-reaction as opposed to reaction.) In other words, remember that you have a good measure of conscious control over resentment, and it's time for you to start watching for the opportunity to exercise that control. Resentment, because it is a wrong, willful way to deal with anything, is eating you up by making you more sensitive, weak, and vulnerable.

Every time you respond to stress, you become aware in the next moment of an increased vulnerability and helplessness that was brought on by your response. It is a good awareness—you *should* be aware of the forces that you are allowing to eat you alive. The trouble is that most of us are too proud to take such an awareness in stride. Instead of wiping the egg off our face with a laugh and resolving to hang onto our "cool" a little better next time, we *resent* being made aware of our loss of control, as though consciousness itself were the problem, and not the key to the solution, which, of course, it is.

You surely do not want to go on being a rotten person, but you must learn to stop resisting the inner knowing that follows on the heels of every wrong reaction. You must realize that your constant evasions and denials, your willful attempts to rewrite the script, are only making matters worse.

It all started with your will to gain power, love, and recognition. Without realizing you were doing it, you have probably been playing God. As a god/creator, you have delighted in creating effects in order to enjoy the reaction of love or hate they evoke in yourself and others.

You must start looking at yourself objectively, with your own understanding, for it is the pure light of realization that saves you—not the learning of principles as they have been enunciated or written by Roy Masters or by anyone else, regardless of how much they may have been esteemed and hallowed by various social institutions. It is only through your own realization that you receive living knowledge from God, the intimate understanding of the way He would have you go, which enables you to repent of your former willfulness and resign yourself to the Divine Will, to become one with it.

To experience this perfect knowing, even for a moment, is to know Reality as a certainty, in a way that you never dreamed possible, and you want to hang onto it forever, perhaps even to share it with others. But don't be too quick to mount the podium, lest you proclaim the good news as your own discovery, take all the credit for it, and puff up in pride. Remember the razor's edge. Guard your newly discovered understanding with quiet humility. Prove it only by living as your Creator would have you live.

When you first wake up to real meaning, the sheer rightness of it might tempt you to work it over on an intellectual level, to analyze it, argue with it (like a devil's advocate) to test it, or freeze-frame it for future use. Be careful. Remember that you have no need to commit Truth to memory. Truth is ever-present to light your path, as long as you are going Truth's way. The simplicity of understanding relieves you of the burden of memory. You are no longer a blind man, trying to remember where everything is as he gropes his way around the house. The light endows you with faith and patience, a quiet knowing that things will change as they should, without your having to know how or why.

Do you see how all your problems have evolved from the original sin of pride? How it invaded your ego at an early age, and set your mind to analyzing and trying to understand the evolving grossness of flesh by its own dark light? Even when you try to be a better person by an effort of will, it is pride that motivates your struggle. The very fact that you struggle shows that you are not ready to be still, to face the truth, to give up your selfish willing.

The ego, in its willfulness, is always in motion, escaping into knowledge for its answers, struggling with symptoms and problems in its effort to know itself as the captain of all it surveys. Pride can effect changes only by interacting with problems and striving to prove its power to conquer and heal, even though its efforts always result in proving the exact opposite. At that point, discovering that it can not create in a "positive" way, it delights in tearing down and destroying in the name of "creation."

Are you constantly looking for sympathy by planting in the

minds of others the kind of "knowledge" that will evoke it, and thus validate your "rightness," despite the fact that you are playing a losing game? Whenever you find yourself reaching for sympathy, your sick soul aquiver with hunger for the soothing lie, realize that you would have no need of the lie if you were living by the light of true understanding. See that your own efforts to make things better are actually making them worse and causing you to sink lower—even in the hierarchy of the world. Who ever respects the loser he is called upon to stroke?

It may be hard to realize that we are doing it, but all of us are creating bigger problems through our struggle to solve existing ones. Like the person looking for sympathy, we are looking for reaction, for or against, "out there," to provide our egos with the challenge they need in order to evolve and manifest their glory in the flesh. We might better spend our energy on bouncing a ball against a wall! If we really wanted solutions, we would look to the stillness within—not out there.

Problems challenge your pride to grow physically and intellectually. As the problem evolves, it stays just ahead of your own need to react and to escape into "growth." Since the problem grew out of your pride's need to develop itself, it is your pride that is threatened and causing your anxiety. But of course, the big problem on the outside helps you to forget the inside guilt that caused it.

"Where would we be without problems?" egomaniacs cry. They would be miserable in a world that had no need of their "solutions" to the problems they are so good at creating. They cannot stand peace. It threatens their system.

You must realize the folly of trying to cure the problems your ego created through its willful selfishness. You have allowed your entire existence to revolve around your emotional need to struggle against reality and escape into a world of illusion, with pride in the driver's seat. Every step you take on this path leads you closer to sickness and death.

The struggle against the problem is as great a sin as the sin that brought on the problem in the first place. For as long as you struggle, you show your unwillingness to surrender your will to God. You keep yourself busy with your efforts to develop as a "god" apart from God, but eventually, you will sink exhausted into the mire of the sickness and hell you have used your "godship" to create.

Now that I have pointed out the way to you, will you go in peace? Or will you continue on the restless road of pride?

8

It's Time to Hang up Your Hang-ups

We are so determined to go on dealing with problems in a way that is guaranteed to create new problems that we are absolutely dead set against seeing that that is exactly what we are doing. It is a fact we can not face, so we either suppress the little flashes of realization that might come to us, or we reject any possibility that we could be working against our own best interest. As a result, things continue to get worse.

Of course, there is a right way to cope with life, but in order to find it, we must first see exactly how we are contributing to our problems by the very efforts we exert to "solve" them. There comes a time in life when we must be willing to take some personal responsibility for the part we play in all the things that are happening to us. We must be objective enough to see the common thread running through our problems, and to realize that they could not possibly fit us so well if we had had nothing to do with their creation.

It all boils down to the uniquely human factor of moral choice. The lower animals enjoy a freewheeling, carefree existence just by doing what comes naturally—by following their instincts. And, as I explained in the last chapter, we could enjoy a similar freedom from care and worry if we lived by the conscience that commits us to the service of our Creator *and of nothing else.* Ah, there's the rub.

Thanks to our having some freedom of choice in our governance, we can incline toward what is fair and sensible or toward what is vain and foolish. All that is basically wrong with us is that we have forgotten—or we have been made to forget, through a series of wrong choices and responses—how to be ourselves. We have somehow allowed ourselves to be changed from what we were meant to be, and this altered self exists in an alien world, out of harmony with what it was intended to be. In order to get back into step with our destiny, we must seek out the original purpose of our creation.

Unfortunately, either we don't know how to reclaim our original identity, or we don't want to know; so we keep falling into a deeper pit, a more problem-fraught existence. From here, we see the problem as the answer and the truth as the real problem. Every foolish thing becomes attractive. Real friends look like enemies to us, and enemies become our "friends." What we are caught up in, in the final analysis, is a rebellion against what is morally right and good for us. We indulge a secret, self-serving love for the evils that support our rebellion against common sense, the selfless way of serving our Creator's purpose. And as long as we insist on sacrificing our lives to a wrong cause, we will be fixated to responding in a wrong way and dramatizing the wrong that has claimed our allegiance. The wrong within will continue to seek refuge in the wrong without, and they will grow together, the one feeding on the other in a symbiotic relationship.

Regardless of the proclamations of William Ernest Henley, the poet, we are not "masters of our fate" and "captains of our soul."

But if we fail to submit to the mastery of good, we shall certainly fall under the control of evil. When we base our lives on what is wrong, what we get is a *sense* of mastery; what is worse, we become slaves of this sense, this illusion.

If we fail to subject ourselves to what is right in our hearts, we fall subject to what is wrong. What makes that wrong impulse so attractive to us? Isn't it the fact that it supports the egotistical notion that we can overcome the Lord we should be serving and rule in His place? Well, we cannot. We were born to serve, not to rule, and if we are not serving God, we are serving evil. The only mastery, and the greatest mastery we could possibly hope to know, is the mastery we gain over our emotions and actions when we cleave to the right way with an unwavering commitment.

We will master nothing until we return our allegiance to Him Who made all things. Until that time, we will remain ever reactive and sensitive to the pressures and pleasures of the world. Furthermore, our need to react to those things will increase because we need their gravitational pull to hold us down in the world of our illusions.

While we manage to do a great deal of wrong to one another, we are never conscious of deliberately "doing wrong." It is only in retrospect that we can see the wrong we have done, if indeed we ever do. At the time of the deed, "doing wrong" is the furthest thing from our thoughts. As a matter of fact, quite often we are not thinking at all because we are completely under the sway of our wrong emotions. To sin, we must literally set conscience aside, and when we do, we become automatons of evil.

Conscience erects a barrier between us and the forbidden world, the world of "highs," of selfish, sensual delights. When we make a willful leap over that barrier, our defection causes us so much uneasiness that we find it necessary to make another leap. We have to find some "cure" for that guilty conscience, and our favorite cure is escape.

As a whole person, you are not even aware that you have a conscience. It bothers you only when you overstep its limits, and then you know it as a painful hindsight. When you are a friend to your conscience, you know it as "foresight," the common sense that keeps you playing by the rules and eschewing temptation. Unfortunately, most of us rarely heed the prompting of conscience because we are seeking freedom from it to be "our own" persons. How is it that we find it so easy to set aside the promptings of conscience, the little flickers of alarm that say "step back"? Well, we just turn our attention away from that inward monitor and fasten it on the outer object of desire that has been tugging at our lower, sensual nature. The object we choose to fixate on may be a selfish goal, a fantasy, a worry, a wallowing in self-pity or in some other self-serving indulgence. Whatever it is, if it can compel our attention, it provides an effective escape from truth.

Whatever grabs and holds our attention contributes to our re-shaping in its own image. Strong appeals to our ego capture our attention and arouse the emotional desires that "free" our concupiscent soul to reach for the satisfactions and promised rewards that are implicit in those appeals. We soon find ourselves living in an altered state of consciousness and experiencing the physiological changes that proclaim our new allegiance.

While it is true that many different concerns can be screaming for our attention at any given time, the fact remains that eventually we have to make a choice; and the minute we focus our attention on one appeal, we automatically exclude the others from our consideration. The one we select to receive our attention will be the one that is most in harmony with the inclination of our soul. The call to virtue is easily overlooked by the self-centered, selfish person with prideful goals. He feels perfectly justified in attending only to those objects and values that will contribute to the evolution of his pride.

The proud man's goal works like the donkey's carrot on the end of a stick. It keeps him motivated and moving as it leads his mind away from reality into a dream world. To focus on a goal is to look at the world with tunnel vision. It enables you to shut out any awareness of your selfishness along with your conscience. You set one goal after another for yourself in order to escape the guilt that your last "success" should have caused you to experience. And as you continue to give in to your fascination with foolish ambition, you fall in consciousness. You become the servant of all you seek to control.

The longer you allow your mind to be enslaved by the wrong way of concentrating and thinking, the more you fear to face the truth that would free you from your fixations. Your pride has depended on them too long for justification and support. You think that if you can keep the world's attention focused on the riches you have amassed, it's possible that no one will notice the little you have *become* in the process. You have been out of touch with your own identity for so long that you are now completely dependent on a reflected image of the one your pride projected onto the world for your own feelings of worth.

Even when you fall ill from your lifestyle, your attention remains fixed "out there." Your proud ego, obsessed by the false hope for a cure, looks to a medicine, a drug, a diet—to *anything* that will eliminate the symptoms while leaving your pride intact to continue evolving. Such a cure would be worth its weight in gold to you because it would pose no threat to your ego. Even your fixation to the idea that such a cure exists constitutes another escape, another means of building your pride. Your fixation, first to this pill, then to that pill, can delude you into thinking that you are improving, partly because the false hope buoys up your pride and partly because it keeps you separate from the conscience that would not hold you guiltless. Of course, when the fix wears off, your pride will once again feel threatened by the truth of your foolishness and by the fact that you are worse off than you were when you reached out for the cure.

If you are hung up on having to protect your pride at all costs you are like the man who, waking up to find his house on fire, blames the blaze on the fact that he woke up. All he has to do to put out the fire is go back to sleep, where he will rest secure in his belief that all is well.

Fixating to anything—wine, women, song, medicine, sports, entertainment—is like going back to sleep as far as the ego is concerned; anything that narrows your vision to the point that you lose sight of the way of truth becomes an addiction, and you will find it impossible to serve your addiction and remain aware and alert at the same time. Something has to go, and it isn't likely to be the excitement of the moment. A common characteristic of all these attention-getters is their ability to make you feel good about yourself while sucking up a little more of your autonomy under cover of each new thrill, and rendering you more dependent on lies for the perpetuation of your illusions.

To survive as a fallen being, you need some drug, some tease, to keep you moving in an orbit beyond reality. Man's first "tease," his original "fixer," the source of his fall into carnal beingness, is woman. She rules over a vast repertoire of escapes and knows full well how to make them available for a man's pleasure taking. Her survival, like that of the politician, depends on her ability to "get under the skin" and become a problem to those she "serves."

The male nature that came into existence through tease now depends on tease for its survival. Remember that anything that tempts also teases because it captures your attention for itself, regardless of what you were concentrating on before you were so pleasantly interrupted. Tease seems to solve the problem of providing some impetus for your ego's growth, but while doing so, it provides you with a bigger problem. The baneful woman is a complete entertainment center in herself, in a manner of speaking. First, she grabs a man's attention with love offerings, but later she keeps him transfixed by a confusing air of inscrutability. She develops a knack for serving him while remaining always just a little beyond the reach of his understanding, and it drives him up the wall.

Remember that anything with the ability to hold your attention will "get" to you and re-create itself in you, thus imparting to you the illusion that it is *you* who are being created for the first time—

the "old you" somehow never existed at all. Escaping into a fascination, therefore, is like waking up in a brand new world as far as your male pride is concerned.

In order to escape the constraints of consciousness, you are unconsciously obliged to empower the tease with the energy it must exert on you in order to keep you at the "right" pitch of excitement. In other words, you continue to give power to the problem, whether it be a person, a place, or a thing, in order to obtain the maximum "good" out of it for the growth of your ego, your pride. So you see that, in a sense, the tease helps to solve one of your problems, the one of providing you with a means of escape from your conscience so that you might enjoy the worldly delights your ego craves for its growth. From the point of view of Reality, of course, you have made the problem worse with all your aiding and abetting. Paradoxically, even though you may think you want to get rid of the problem, especially if all it is providing you is the agony of self-righteous judgment, you are powerless to stop feeding it and making it grow—your proud ego needs its challenge for the sake of its own development as a prouder and prouder ego. The next time you find yourself soliciting a friend's sympathy by bellyaching about your problems, just watch how the very act of doing so is fattening up those problems, along with your hungry ego.

No matter how often you allow yourself to get hooked by the false promises of "fixers," and wind up drained and worse off than you were before, you keep hoping that the next one will really have the power to rid you of guilt and shame. So you keep looking for the ultimate "fix," the one that will put you on top. Through all these fixations, you are developing into a wrong kind of man, the kind of man who looks to the wrong kind of woman for his completion. By the light of what I have been telling you, do you see how your fixation to a woman might actually create in her the need to serve you up bigger and bigger helpings of the love/hate tease you are so obviously craving? If she had no problem before you came along, she certainly has one now. And you keep giving it new power because your guilty, violated self gravitates to the ground of tease for escape and support. (When a man looks for a wife, he looks for the same selfless acceptance he got from his mother. Whether he realizes it or not, his mother will serve as the criterion in his choice of a mate.)

By escaping into the tease of problems, you keep renewing the creature self, the beast man, the devil's own pawn; then, when you get a glimpse of what is really happening to you, your ego compels you to escape again, this time into "survival." By fixating on survival, you continue to reject truth in favor of the lie, thus adding to the legacy of hell that you inherited. When the grim demands of survival begin to pall, you seek relief in yet another distraction, in recreation. Our word "recreation" literally means re-creation, a kind of renewing of the fallen man through excitement, intrigue, and entertainment.

Some people are content to live their entire lives as helpless pawns of the manipulators who know how to turn them on emotionally. Their only purpose in life is to be happy, and their idea of goodness is to make others happy. Reality is a concept they can deal with only in the simplest materialistic terms. Tell them that they are running out of control and they'll answer "You must be kidding!" Obviously, you are not one of those, or you would not be reading this book. You may realize that you are not in control of your life, that you are being manipulated against your will, and that there is little you can do about it with your own effort. You want to find the relationship with your Creator that will get you back on track—and enable you to do and to live in the way He designed you to do and to live, cheerfully, and without effort. Let me help you find your way to the way.

No amount of will power can enable you to get rid of your hang-ups, your fixations to the people and things that are causing all your problems. First, you must realize that there are two ways to give your attention to anything, and the distance between them is as thin as a razor's edge. The one leads to a hypnotic state, and the other leads to the meditative state. The one you will find yourself in will depend on the way you have fixed your attention—whether you have thrown yourself into it, body and soul, and thereby have become *subject* to the person or the discipline you were following—or whether you have managed to keep your soul so focused on the Most High for guidance that you have managed to remain *objective*, thereby leaping over the middle man and availing yourself of the objective state of consciousness to which he was pointing instead of allowing yourself to get caught up with the "pointer. " Needless to say, the person who has always been aware of the duality of his nature will find it easier to remain objective than will the person who sees himself as "all of a piece" and identifies himself as all that is contained within his body "package."

Whichever way you focus your attention, hypnotically or meditatively, you may experience a sensation of freedom, but the nature of that free feeling will depend on your secret intent. If you were so caught up with the idea that the fixer could "fix" you that you relinquished all responsibility for the outcome into the hands of the fixer (the person or the experience itself), you will feel free all right, but it will be the freedom of a slave who no longer has to worry about his actions because he no longer has any control over them. Like Esau, you will have traded your birthright for something of no intrinsic value. You are "'free" of the inhibitions of conscience, so you can do whatever "you want to do, but you have indentured yourself to whatever "freed" you. What you *think* you want to do may have no connection with what your original consciousness would have had you do, but you do it anyway. Of course, you do not see that you are a slave because when you accepted the false "freedom," you rejected the true freedom that is found only in Truth, the perspective that would have made you aware of what you were about to give up for the sake of a false sense of freedom. If you had remained committed to the Truth within, it would have saved you, but you were too anxious to escape responsibility, so you took the "easy" way out.

I hope that I have convinced you of the importance of having a right intent in everything you do, but especially in this matter of giving attention to the people and things around you—including my teaching. In the beginning, you may find that you are caught up with me hypnotically for a season, but no great harm will be done if you see that you are, and continue to readjust your focus on the truth until you arrive at your own objective state of consciousness.

You will be able to tell when you are being caught up hypnotically by the way things affect you emotionally. If your heart starts to beat faster while you are watching a movie, or when you catch sight of a particularly appealing member of the opposite sex, see that your attention is getting involved in a selfish, egocentric, and unhealthy way. Whenever you find yourself getting emotionally excited, see it as a sign of danger, a clear indication that you are falling into a hypnotic fixation, and pull back until you can see things in their proper perspective.

Of course, if you are able to pull away from emotional excitement, you will be happy to see your ability to do so as evidence of your right intent, but you must stay on guard lest you puff up in pride and fall again.

Above all, don't expect any help from the people around you in this matter of aspiring to maintain an objective state of consciousness. Most people think that emotionality, the stuff of pride, is what makes the world go around. They revel in unhealthy fixations so much that they actually fear the calm, objective state, preferring to cultivate and wallow in their lowly, animal sensory experiences. Prepare to be given a wide berth as you move among them. Old friends will withdraw their support of *your* ego as you wisely start to withdraw your support of *theirs.*

Emotion, you see, derives its power to hold your attention with so much magnetic force from the fact that it helps your ego to feel secure in its sin. The "fix," whatever it is that captures your attention, creates the emotion, but the emotion, in turn, helps to reinforce and strengthen the "fix." Emotion draws your consciousness away from conflict, and evokes in you a sensual, no-holds-barred type of growth. It is the stimulus that keeps you going to the theater, to ball games, and other diversions. If your own life has your pride on a starvation diet, you can always fill up by identifying with the emotional ups and downs of others. Through every emotional uplift, your selfish soul feels reborn. It hears lies as Truth, and clings to them for Life itself.

Anything we can say about the dangers of emotionality shows up most clearly in the man-woman relationship. A man looks to this relationship for blessed relief from the feelings of self-consciousness he experiences when he involves himself completely in sensual excitement. Egocentric fixation of any kind awakens the sleeping giant of sensuality that overwhelms the real man and lowers the quality of his real life. To escape the guilt of it, he feels compelled to refixate again and again. The guiltier a man becomes, the more he fears being alone, or in any position where he might be forced to see things objectively, so he depends on his "fixes" for his very survival.

Until you are ready to surrender utterly to the purpose for which you were created, you will be looking only to the ways of the world for your survival. You will continue to table-hop from one fixer to the next for your emotional feeling of security. Through all the hypnotic fixations that feed you delusions of life (Man, *this is living!*) and of worth, you are slowly handing over your soul and becoming a creature of darkness, fearful of the real freedom of truth's way, "secure" only in an illusion, a fixed emotional belief system. Either you don't know, or you don't want to know, how to unfixate your consciousness from its life of "self" worship through pleasure.

When you concentrate, or fixate *away* from Reality, toward goals and pleasures, you temporarily forget the condemnation of conscience and the ultimate penalty of death. Instead, you feel the stirrings of a new self-righteous, earthy creature life. You trade your true and eternal life for a selfish ego life.

When we look around us at all the various "lifestyles," we tend to think that there are many ways to live a life, but in reality there are only two. Either we are committed to the right way of God or the wrong way of evil, and a commitment to one renders us oblivious to the other.

The ambitious and prideful are "dead," alive only in the sense that they experience the evolution of a creature self by way of tease fixations. Through their fixations, they continually rededicate themselves to selfishness, while stubbornly denying the truth of the fact that they are sick unto death, despite their proclamations of joy in the "good life," the sensuous life of pleasure.

By fixating through time and space, you eventually discover the evil standing behind matter, and at that point of descent, you could become fascinated with evil itself. Your guilt-ridden, restless mind can become terrified of being still, thanks to its having escaped into its own morbidity. Long after it has forgotten how to succeed by having fixated to goals, it can be left with the fixation to failure by way of resentment and hatred. All fixations, pleasant and uplifting, or unpleasant and morbid, serve the purpose of pride.

Fixations exert a powerful hold over you because your emotional identification with them relieves you of guilt; also, when you abandon yourself to their leadership and stroking, you provide your ego with a rich ground for the evolution of its selfishness and pride. Of course, you don't want to give them up—they are vital to your pride's survival. Until you are ready to commit yourself to your Creator, you dare not be free and objective, for if you were to step into the light, you would see the false belief and the false self it has planted in you in all their ignoble destructiveness. You will want to kill what has been killing you, and to kill the proud self, if it is the only self you know, is to die. And you *must* die to sin if you are ever to live by Truth. It is a death you won't mind at all, because you will no longer care about the pleasures and rewards of a life of sin.

For God's sake, for your own sake, hang up those hang-ups!

9

Stress:
Get Ready to Live Without It

You have probably been hiding behind your "fixes" all your life, using them to make the reality of evil "go away." You cling to them like the lifesavers they are as long as they represent all that you want and need out of life. When they pull the rug out from under you or fail you in some way, and you start to get a glimpse of what a shambles your life is in without their support, you panic. You feel that you are being punished or cursed for not having been sufficiently wholehearted in the service of your "fixers" and you throw yourself on their mercy once again— not to heal you of your shortcomings but to provide you with the pleasurable feelings and sensations that will enable you to forget their existence, along with the rest of reality.

Until you are ready to face the Light and abide by its dictates, you will undoubtedly be caught up with ego-serving goals, women to support those goals, drinking, drugs, and finally, violence. As an egocentric fool you are terrified of female rejection because you are inherently dependent on the guile and the total acceptance through which the female transmits the lie and its lifestyle. When a woman rejects you she frees your consciousness to experience the terror that comes with waking up and realizing what a fool you have become through your "using" in the name of "loving." But the chances are that you will soon seek another escape in another fixation, such as worry about the state of the world or some tedious, time-absorbing study— anything to get away from facing the problem of self.

Any happiness, security, salvation, or cure that you can "realize" through another person, place, institution, or thing constitutes a fixation and is therefore a form of corruption. Once you are hooked, the "benevolent" sources of your corruption can convince you that if you dare to give up their treatment, or leave their church, or give up their booze or their music, you will fall prey to all manner of tragedy. But you are already mired in tragedy, thanks to your dependence on these false sources of security. This is something you usually fail to realize until you have let go of the fixation; and even then, the wicked person or group can often turn your thinking around to make you believe that the horror has just begun, whereas you are really just beginning to discover its presence.

The truth is that you never really had security, well-being, and happiness. Your corruptors actually robbed you of the very things they pretended to give you; and as long as you cling to pride's way, you will go on believing you are *getting* while you are being *got*. Should you catch a glimpse of Truth, it would threaten your sensuous emotional existence and drive you closer to your corruptors and vices.

When a man looks too longingly and needfully at a woman, he bestows upon her a god-like power, a power that the wrong within her seizes upon hungrily and uses to fixate him to her for the excitement his pride is craving. The way he gawks at her cries out to her dark, primeval "need to be needed," and the "need" that she serves in him is the further evolution of his pride. A part of the woman enjoys the power, especially if she never knew she had it, and the attention she is receiving may well be the only attention and "love" she will ever know. But another part of the woman is appalled at the hell rising in the man for her stroking and turning him into an irresponsible male animal, a devotee to her indwelling evil, even as she is devoted to his beast. What a hell they are creating for themselves and their family by feeding the twin monsters of pride and power. They are trapped in a joyless game—she, teasing him with the alternate granting and withholding of the tidbits his pride demands, and he, resenting his inability to stop snapping at them. It is a game for which there is no happy ending, no resolution, until the man sees his need to tune in to the one true Source of power for his motivation. Only then will he be able to extend to the woman the ultimate "fix" of divine love, the kind of attention that can not be controlled or manipulated, but is given freely in the service of good. It corrects evil by forbearing to use it.

Remember, always, the importance of watching the way you are giving your attention to the people and things around you, those instantaneous, automatic reactions to stress that signal where you are really coming from—the reactions that catch you red-handed, in a manner of speaking. Others see them and some may even applaud your wrong reactions, but you must see them by the light of Truth and repent of them on the spot, taking whatever measures are appropriate to seeing that justice prevails.

Suppose, for example, your children make a play for your attention by starting to engage in a forbidden activity and it makes you mad. "Put that hammer down," you scream, "and go find something else to do." Do you think that your angry reaction will make better children of them? Or will it make them worse? Of course you already know the answer. The adult's interrupted activity is rarely so important that he can't take a few moments to give the children the right kind of attention they crave and direct them to a better activity, perhaps even join them in it for a few minutes. Dealing with others resentfully, or too sympathetically, is a sure-fire way of escalating the problem: they will get more proficient at "setting you off" and you will rise to greater heights of self-righteous "correction."

As for the overly sympathetic response, it is the one you use to protect yourself from getting upset, the self-serving armor you try to keep in place at all times in order to disable others from rejecting you. You are too needful of their approval. If you are operating in this mode, you give in to your child or you try to put a better face on his misbehavior. Of course, he probably sees right through you and can't really love you for your slavish insecurity, but he certainly learns to exploit the advantage that your need for his love is giving him. You teach him to tease for what he wants. And when he rewards you for giving in, his purring approval increases the pride you take in your weakness. As you get more proficient at using the child to serve your pride, he gets more proficient at exploiting your weakness.

Surely you see by now the dangers inherent at both extremes. Compulsive attention, springing either from the extreme of love or the extreme of hate, will always bring out the worst in others to serve the worst in you. Remember that love-fixation cannot save you from hate-fixation. Each extreme leads back to the other and evolves internal sicknesses, along with external tragedies, for both the "fixer" and the "fixed." Obviously, it behooves us all to find the middle ground of common sense and prepare ourselves to live from it in each moment.

You must learn how to give your attention out of a conscious center of awareness, patiently, untainted by any personal feeling whatsoever. Only the attention that springs from a pure source can convey a healing love to others. Unfortunately, until now, you have probably been unable either to give or to know that kind of loving, patient attention because you (and everyone around you) are caught up in your own ego's need to use those to whom you are drawn by some form of selfish fascination.

You do see, don't you, that wrong attention—that is, the kind of attention that is based on love/hate feelings—is a form of use? Until you have been purged of your sick need for the world's stroking you will be cut off from the Divine love that will free you from your need to use and will enable you to look at your loved ones through different eyes, truly loving eyes. Under the governance of real love you will be able to break away from your sick fixations and pay proper attention to the problems outside, if only by keeping them outside and not letting them in.

Let's look at some of the fixations that are claiming your attention so completely that they are standing between you and your God-given consciousness:

1. *Study*. Be careful not to concentrate so hard, with so much emotional investment that you make a god of learning and intellectual achievement. If you feel driven to learn you may be using the acquisition of knowledge as an escape from the more important reality considerations with which you should be concerning yourself. Remember that anything you use as an escape corrupts and creates an addiction to the source of corruption, whatever it might be.

2. *Guilt*. Guilt, regardless of the sin that evoked it, deepens your involvement with fixations. Nobody wants to feel guilty, but you make the mistake of thinking that the only way you can escape the guilt is to justify somehow the person or thing that induced the guilt and exalt its importance in your life. How can you possibly be guilty of becoming too involved with your pets or your music when obviously, as you insist to the world and to yourself, they are your whole life? Well, they shouldn't be, and the part of you that you tried to leave behind knows it.

3. *Emotional Longing*. When others display emotional feeling for you, even though the emotion might be phony, you tend to reflect the same feeling for them in a kind of monkey-see-monkey-do reaction. And as the soul becomes fixated on emotional stroking it falls even farther from reality and becomes

more needful of emotion, even to the point of feeling grateful toward the corruptor who initiated the fall.

Remember that whenever the soul is seduced it falls to emotion, and when we use that emotion to pull the soul away from realizing the truth of its fall we add sin to sin, thus creating a larger field to nourish the feelings of "life" our emotions are giving us. Fixation creates emotion and emotion creates fixation and before we know it we are caught up in a vicious cycle of compulsion. Even the emotion you use to try to break the cycle, usually anger or resentment, will give greater power to the corruptor. For instance, when you become angry at one of your bad habits, like overeating or smoking, the very anger you feel will drive you deeper into the habit for relief. Any use of emotion to distract the soul from its awareness of guilt will give more power to the fixation until it becomes an overpowering compulsion. Even when you seek relief from morbid preoccupations and internal conflicts by distracting yourself with the kinds of experiences and imaginings that arouse pleasant emotions in you, you are only making matters worse. Adding emotion to emotion can never solve the problems that our emotional reactions created. True, most of us, until we begin to see the light, enjoy our emotional confusions because of the feelings of life and security we draw from them. We seldom back off for a more objective look at what they are doing to us until the pain of them has driven us to the breaking point.

4. *Lust*. A selfish desire for anything, be it love, money, success, home-ownership, anything at all, is what we know as "ambition," but a better name for it is a "fixation to failing." You allow your excessive desire to become famous, successful, or glorious to distract you from seeing the folly of putting your selfish ambition ahead of wanting to find the unique and proper place for which you were destined. True, you very well might be marked for fame and glory, but it should come about as the result of your having done the right thing with your talents in each moment, in accordance with your principled common sense. When it comes

about naturally in that way, it's like icing on the cake and you can really be grateful for having been so well graced by your Creator. But when your lust for success is strong enough to overpower principle, you will find that you have been "got" by all you tried to get, and even if you do get what you went after, it won't look all that good to you. As soon as you reach the finish line, your conscience will have a chance to take over, and your guilt will spoil the taste of "victory." You might even set about to destroy the very thing you have fought so hard to get. And if you are a confirmed loser, you will just tamp your guilt down into the lower depths of your consciousness and set out in pursuit of a bigger and better goal.

The person who is intent on getting ahead and "making something" of himself fixates his attention on one goal after another in order to free his ego from the inhibition of conscience. He keeps himself much too "busy" to realize that each goal is another sin, another way to fail. The habit of fixating is the real sin, of course. Practiced daily, it tears you a little further away from the soul's center as it re-commits you to a life of selfish greed. When we allow our attention to dwell on wrong goals we lose sight of the wrong that is growing up within ourselves. And until we have stifled our conscience entirely the little bit of awareness that nips at our heels makes us afraid to stop and ponder. The mind must keep moving and reaching out, enslaving itself to one distraction after another in order to free itself from the awareness of its failing. It dares not stop long enough to let the truth catch up, lest it stand convicted.

Your ambition has caused you to reject God by making gods of those who have served your pride. You have made the dream life real and the real life a dream.

You can even become addicted to the sweat-of-the-brow work to which the Lord has committed us by fixating to it too eagerly and working too hard for the sake of profit, even when that profit is just another pat on the back, another morsel of pride food. Or you might be using your fixation to over-achieving as a means of escaping the stress of your home situation. You might actually hate the work itself, but it gives you extra time away from home and you "season" its value to you as an escape with the spice of self-righteousness, seeing yourself as a martyr, bravely shouldering the cross he is forced to bear.

The proud ego is a creature of fixation. It must "fix" to survive as a proud ego. A man works on his boat day and night because he identifies with it to such an extent that when he is beautifying the boat he feels that he is beautifying himself. A man can never do enough for anything he lusts after because he is really doing it for himself.

Anything you fixate to, whether it is work or even listening to music, provides a distraction, an escape into pride food and feelings of false happiness. How could a virtuous person be truly happy while lapping up the secondhand outpourings of some drug-crazed rock star or, for that matter, the harmonious strains of a symphony orchestra, if he were to let them get past his ear, to invade and flatter his soul.

Through our fixations we are all unconsciously creating our own problems in order to evolve the ego beast. And the problems we create are the very breath of life to our proud egos. We love to cultivate wickedness in the name of goodness because only evil can serve our complex needs for distraction and support. We enjoy hating evil, and we enjoy being stroked by evil. And, as the Bible says, our love of the world (evil) makes us enemies of God.

Loving or hating, you give power to the problem (or to the evil) so that the problem, person, or thing can deaden your conscience and stimulate the animal side of your nature. When you are a problem-centered person, you are constantly reacting to any challenge to your ego, and it is that reaction that gives the evil its power to evolve itself in you, to the point that it takes over your identity. The problem grows ever bigger, with greater power to tease and to draw your attention. The more guilty you become, the more power you give to the evil to free you from your guilt and help you grow in pride.

One might think that the object of reacting to a problem is to solve it. Not so! We react to the problem in order to *cultivate* it and absorb its stress. Remember that pride is completely mad. Are you beginning to see how mad you are becoming yourself? Do you see how you need to react (wrongly) to everything? It has been your way of keeping the wheels turning, filling you with a sense of growing through your emotional connectedness to the world around you.

Even now, you are loath to give up the rich emotional mulch you are thriving in. You don't want the friends who have been supporting and entertaining you to start seeing you as cold and heartless, as you very well know they *will*, if you dare to stop playing the "love" game with them. But until you are ready to commit your life to God, let the attachments fall where they will, you cannot overcome the emotions that connect you to what you think of as life itself.

You will never be able to live a simple, innocent life as long as you use emotion to preserve the life of your ego. If you were to lead a simple, happy, unstressed life—and you could, you know— where would you get your sense of accomplishment and growth? You need evil to react to, to escape into, and to evolve from. Reacting to stress, you reinforce the life that comes through the stress. You are addicted to the stress that corrupted you and triggered the process of change in you as the result of some long-ago, long-forgotten trauma.

You cannot resolve your problems because they are a necessary evil to you. Haven't you ever noticed how similar they all are and how well they fit you? Many people have to be sick all the time; if one doctor won't operate, they shop around until they find one who will. They are too prideful, too guilty, to face reality, so they wallow in the challenge of the diseases and operations from which they draw comfort. They even take pride in the noble struggle they are putting up against cancer, instead of repenting of the sin that caused it in the first place. What fools they are; what fools we all are!

We can live a week or so without water, but not one minute without the comfort of lies and intrigue. The whole world is bogged down in the problems of its own making. In the process of finding wrong solutions to problems, we sink more deeply into our misery as we add to our guilt and damnation. It would appear that the underlying unconscious need in all men and women is to make life complicated.

A sick ego needs a sick climate in which to grow and to evolve. And we certainly do our best to provide such a climate for ourselves. All of us, as individuals and as societies, are constantly preoccupied with some kind of war or intrigue—it can be scientific, intellectual, domestic, economic, or political. Yet all the while the "problem" we keep trying to "solve" is the unwanted nagging of our own conscience. To get away from it, we evolve a strange and alien identity with which to override the nagging conscience, and we take a strong, ready-for-battle, defensive pride in this false identity we have created for ourselves.

Let's take another look at the frenzied "solvers" of social problems. Have their answers ever really solved anything, or have they created even bigger problems to solve? Does not the survival of big government depend on a constant proliferation of problems? You know it does. But so does your big fat ego.

Sick governments are simply the extension of the sick egos behind them. They cannot and will not use the healing balm of common sense because it is not self-serving from the point of view of their composite ego. Observe how the bureaucrats feed their fat egos on the problems they create, how their "remedies" invariably result in higher taxes and more offices, thus forcing the citizens to reward them with more attention and greater power. The unhealthy attention you get from a politician resembles the attention you get from any con man or flirtatious, guileful woman. They all seem to be interested in improving the quality of your life, but their efforts inevitably result in more power for themselves and more social unrest for the rest of us. Do you see how it parallels what is going on in your own family?

Bureaucracies, like all other forms of corruption, thrive on their ability to provoke you with tease. The people who support them enjoy the close relationship with power, even as they gripe about their powerlessness *vis-à-vis* those to whom they have given that power. In the same spirit, men continually delight in putting women down, but despite their announced displeasure with the shortcomings of the opposite sex, they continue to get married. Fallen men are not fit to live in a perfect world; they are fit only for a world of filth, dirt, slime, and madness—the outward expression of what they are inside.

All social ills evolve out of the collective spirit of a world filled with unloved females. International conflicts, war, and violence of all kinds are manifestations of the love/hate fixations we have with our leaders that hold our attention away from the mess that they themselves have made of our lives. The greater their sin, the more warlike we will become, and they know it. So, to avoid our wrath, a leader will keep our attention focused on the wickedness of a common enemy. By doing so he holds our attention away from the truth about our own internal problems, including the ways in which our leaders are complicating our lives.

The truth is that you, like your leaders, are gradually becoming infected by the very evil you are reacting to, whether your reaction is one of hate or of love. You are disabling yourself from the ability to see what is happening to you by not calming down and sitting still long enough to let the truth catch up to what is going on within you.

You always feel so justified, so virtuous, when you hate an enemy, and it is the same proud self-righteousness, felt collectively, that challenges a country to evolve. Unfortunately, the evolution that takes place leads inexorably to your developing within yourself the very evil you were so proudly fighting. Remember the old saw: "It takes a thief to catch a thief"? No wonder a soldier returning home from battle goes off the deep end when he sees that his own country has become infested with the evil he was fighting.

Because he has a war-centered, violence-oriented identity, the traumatized veteran is forced to relive the battlefield episodes in his mind, lest he turn his need for violence against his family and friends. The violent creature of sin that he has become needs to fixate to some outside evil, even if he has to conjure it up from the past, in order to keep the secret of what he has become, both from himself and from his friends. His need for stress has tricked his soul into playing host to the alien within that is ever intent on fighting the external conspiracy in a wrong way.

Do you see now that the only "problem" you are solving by your addiction to stress is that of assuring the survival of the alien being within you, through the destruction of everything good around it? At this point, you may actually think that it would be impossible to live happily in a stress-free orientation to the world, but the fact is that you will not know pure joy until you stop reacting to stress.

10

How Emotion Enslaves Us
to Our Comforters

E motion drugs us into believing that emotion is right for us, so right that we cannot question the emotional way of life any more than the drug addict can, or will, question his use of drugs to support his ego. Some people get away with existing emotionally. They add emotion to emotion to keep from seeing their mistakes—even those that are the direct result of their having reacted emotionally. They manage to see what they want to see and hear what they want to hear without ever touching drugs. But some of us cannot escape so wholeheartedly into our emotions.

Some of us, even though we may be just as badly caught up in an emotional way of life, are a little too sensitive and aware to be able to play the game of emotion with the same gusto. We may not know what is bugging us, but we know that something is, and we don't want any part of it. Some of these finely-tuned souls, alas, are the ones who turn to drugs or some other form of addiction for relief. And those others, the emotion addicts, help drive them to it!

Because emotion acts as an opiate on our minds, we rarely see that our habit of reacting emotionally to every person and thing and circumstance is the cause of all our personal and interpersonal problems. We are aware only of the anxiety and pain it produces in us, and how desperately we crave to be relieved of the symptoms. When something appears to provide us with that relief, we identify it as being something "good" for us, of course, and it rarely occurs to us to ask whether it really got to the root of the problem.

Addiction may begin with some simple remedy, like candy, aspirin, or a doctor's prescription. Or just a little drink to be "sociable." From then on, it's just a matter of degree, and we go down one step at a time, adjusting to each level as we come to it—no questions asked. We rationalize every step of the way. Our pills and snorts are our friends—they make us feel secure. If a little is good, then a little more is better yet; so our taste for them increases, and as we spend more time on gratifying that taste, we allow the problems of everyday life to pile up in such profusion that we may turn to hard drugs to escape them.

Drug addiction is rooted in emotion, the mother of *all* addiction, the original drug that dulls the mind to reality and causes us to make one foolish decision after another. When we allow ourselves to become emotionally excited or upset, we cannot see clearly, so we blunder our way through life. Even though we manage to see that we have been caught up in a world of emotion, it's still the only world we know and we don't know how to stop it long enough to get off.

When we have been turned on emotionally, we lack the power to turn ourselves off. Any counterpressure simply highlights our helplessness, and we feel as though we were driving with the brakes on. We may reach for a drug to calm ourselves down and assure us that all is well with us—but it is not. As long as we remain subject to emotional pressures and rely on drugs to make them bearable, the weaker we get, until finally we need the drugs to turn us on and to turn us off.

All the "turn-ons" and "turn-offs," from emotion to the innocent filling of a doctor's prescription to full-blown hard drug addiction—all uppers and downers keep us from honest self-examination. They stand between us and the right answer. Even when we are inclined to cry out for help, the wrong answer intervenes with a false promise of relief, and it stifles the cry. From the little old lady who soothes her hemorrhoids with suppositories to the aspirin popper, we are all drug addicts. The differences are only a matter of degree. We are all soothing pains that we never should have had. Can the blind in society lead the blind?

We have all been emotionalized, whether we like to admit it or not, by some long-forgotten trauma. Early in our lives, father or mother either dealt with us too harshly or pulled on our heartstrings in a seductive way that upset us and pulled us off balance. Ever since that time we have managed to become involved with people who turn us on in the same way and we are at the mercy of their moods. We even need them because we have learned to need the motivation they provide. Whatever the emotion they arouse in us, even if it be intense hatred, we may be sure that their ability to do so had a great deal to do with our having chosen them as friends in the first place. And it's no coincidence if they remind us of one of our parents.

Emotions, like the drugs that reactivate them, make us feel alive and right, and they blind us to the knowledge of our failings. When we vent our anger and impatience on the wrongs of another, we forget that there is anything wrong with ourselves. And when we feel that we actually "love" someone, we bask in our ability to do so as we assume our "rightful" place among the angels of heaven.

Anyone or anything that lifts our spirits emotionally also distorts our thinking. Many celebrities are literally drunk on applause, so slavishly addicted to it that they hear it ringing in their ears all the time, drowning out any more realistic assessment of their talents. While anger lifts our spirits in one way, false love, praise, lifts them in another way. Any emotion provides us with a distorted view of reality that can involve us in a not-so-funny comedy of errors.

All our false loving and hating, sometimes felt for the same person at the same time, literally tears us apart and causes us to deteriorate as human beings. In time, the turn-on value provided by our "regulars" may no longer provide our failing ego with the security it craves; so we seek out someone or something to recharge our batteries with fresh excitement. And each experience we claim for ourselves also lays claim to us. It is our "friend" because it makes our ego feel good, secure, and right, as though we had never strayed. Under the spell of emotion, we can see nothing wrong with emotion, any more than a person under the influence of drugs can see anything wrong with drugs. We cannot see the fist that has closed over us because it has shut out our light.

Whoever and whatever violates us emotionally makes us dependent on the source of the violation, and we mistake the unnatural need it fosters in us for a natural one. We get hung up on liking and being liked, needing and being needed (in the name of love, of course), and we fail to notice that we are stooping lower all the time for the people and things we choose to fill those needs in our life. So the "groovy" new friends who delight us with their tricky new devices lead us by imperceptible degrees away from reason, into a world of rationale and confusion, and we fall prey to philosophies that pander to our excuse-needful ears.

Not only do we need drugs to turn us on or off—we also need rage. Once we discover that there is nothing like a towering rage to get us "off and running"—maybe even to work on time—we begin to see its value as a source of motivation and we therefore conclude that it's "right" to be angry. So we keep looking for things to be angry about until we drain our environment of its gripe value. Finally, we may drink ourselves under the table in order to forget what all that hating has done to us. Then all the wicked people come homing in on the wave length of our emotions to cheer us up, feast on us, and abuse us.

Every externally-triggered emotion is a primitive, dehumanizing drug that will lead to the use of chemicals when our human contacts are no longer able to turn us on with a strong enough force, or when we see that there is something wrong about working out our destructive emotions on other people. Either way, we're upset and frustrated, and we turn to drugs in the hope that they will restore us to our former dignity and self-control. We fail, of course, because dignity and self-control are strictly an inside job. The illusion of peace that we get from drugs has nothing to do with real dignity. As a matter of fact, the addict finally sacrifices all human values for the false peace he finds in his drugs. As he falls to lower levels, the things he has to do to relieve his pain and buy forgetfulness are so bizarre that he has to think of even more bizarre things to do in order to forget what he has already done.

Many psychologists, in order to justify their own emotionality, advise their patients to vent their emotions and avoid painful repression. If we follow that advice, however, the price of our own relief will be a greater emotional problem for our family. They take on our problem by reacting to us and the way they react to us breathes new energy into our problem. It would appear that we are all veritable time bombs and we not only don't know how to defuse ourselves—we don't even know that we're about to go off. And this sorry state of affairs could have been avoided if we had not allowed our moods and feelings to be affected by others in the first place.

Now we must find our way back to a state of dignity and self-control that we can't even remember having, thanks to our having been pulled off our natural center so early in life. On top of that, few of us can really see ourselves objectively because we are all addicted to something. And whatever that something is, we cannot see our addiction to it as an addiction—partly because it is so exciting to us and partly because we look on the relief it gives us as such a "simple pleasure."

Once we allow something to disturb us we learn to need the disturbing presence as a turn-on, even though we may have no real tolerance for it as a human being. We may blow a fuse, or we may not, but if we don't we feel the pain of suppression. At such times we may find ourselves reaching for an old "friend," or even a new one, to make life bearable and pleasant again—to help us forget what we have done, felt, and imagined under the spell of our emotions.

When we blow off steam we pass our emotional problems on to our children. And if we forbear to explode we implode and make a mess of our own psyches. We may soon find ourselves spending so much time and money on our efforts to repair the damage that we can no longer relate properly to the members of our family. We find the relative innocence of our children particularly disturbing because it contrasts so sharply with our own emotional turmoil. Their light is so blinding to us that we feel unconsciously compelled to put it out by doing some unfair petty thing to upset them and whittle them down to our own low level. Sometimes we see how wrong we are in our emotional dealings with our children and sometimes we do not. Either way, whether we baited them deliberately, or whether we escaped seeing the harm we were doing under the spell of our emotions, we provided our children with the trauma they needed to start them off on the same road to misery and oblivion.

This little drama, enacted daily in every home in the nation, has created an unholy tension in our entire society. Because human adrenalin is flowing so freely everywhere, some of us are looking to large-scale social reforms for solutions to the problem, but our common sense should tell us that social action is incapable of solving a problem that begins, and has to end, in the tender psyches of individuals.

The problem of addiction—any kind of addiction—is basically a problem of emotionality. If we could handle our feelings we would automatically be impervious to pills, pot, or whatever. But we are so conditioned to look on our emotions as "only natural" that we are as helpless as the drug addict when it comes to tracing the problem to its root. If we could blink the emotion out of our eyes, even for a few minutes, we could surely see that our habit of giving in to our emotions is what is making us wrong—so wrong that we need our drugs to keep us oblivious to our deterioration as human beings.

In other words, our lack of self-control and our inability to discipline our emotions form the groundwork for all our addictions. If we knew how to control our emotions and stand up to stress with true inner composure we would have no need for artificial pacifiers of any kind. We would have a built-in immunity to addiction.

The more we react to life emotionally the farther we get away from reason, and when our actions cease to be motivated by sound reason we fall prey to guilt and anxiety feelings. (As well we should!) When a person has lost touch with the real way to overcome his reactions to stress he turns in desperation to anything that will make him feel happy, right, and calm. He will reach for cigarettes, drugs, alcohol—anything—to quiet his guilt feelings. And because he bases his sense of rightness on *feeling* right he grows to need more artificial support for those feelings. Remove that support, whatever it is, and he experiences the full impact of his separation from reason—the very thing he was using his addiction to conceal. The guiltier he is, the more drug he needs to ease his guilt and dull his awareness of the faulty emotional reactions that continue to demoralize him, even while he is under the influence of the drug.

The pleasure we derive from relieving the pain of guilt closely resembles divine forgiveness in its effect on us, except that it doesn't force us to experience humiliation or humility—and it certainly does not forgive us. It merely removes the awareness of transgression from our consciousness. The greater the problem, the greater the pleasure in the contrast of relief and the more beneficent the drug appears to be. Drugs actually become substitute religious experiences because they make us feel so good, so free from guilt. But that kind of freedom is not really free because it depends on the drug for its continuance. In order to hang onto the feeling of being "saved" the user must surrender himself to the drug completely. Soon he centers his whole existence around the drug, the source of his "salvation," and he will do anything to maintain his relationship with it. To desert the drug, the savior, would be a sacrilege—a greater guilt than the one he was running from in the first place—or so it seems to his drug-clouded consciousness.

Once they start, people cannot stop using drugs without feeling guilty for having failed their "god." They look to their physical or chemical experiences to relieve them of the guilt they would feel if they were to take a sober look at themselves. Nevertheless, there *are* users who would gladly learn the secret of self-control (not to be confused with suppression) if they only knew how to go about it.

The Foundation of Human Understanding teaches a simple technology to start people on the road to self-discipline, and among the drug addicts and alcoholics who have used it successfully, withdrawal symptoms have been practically nonexistent. The moment a sincerely searching individual learns this technique he is able to meet the next moment, and the next, with composure. He begins to look forward to the encounters with life that once terrified him and as he meets each one successfully he gains ground as a re-humanized being.

A person uses drugs to dull the knowledge of his failing under stress and to blunt his ability to react in the future. But when he learns to approach life correctly he discovers that it is possible to meet life without failing. The true joy he experiences as a result of this discovery casts out the pain that once caused him to seek pleasures. Reality suddenly looks good to him and he is eager to meet all the challenges life has to offer because he is no longer the victim of his experiences. He can go through experiences, no matter how ugly, without letting the experiences go through him. He begins to be his own man.

All addictions have one thing in common: they satisfy your egocentric need to feel right when you are not. People who do not have your best interest at heart, though they appear to, will trade on your needs and encourage them, even sympathize with them, when they believe you to be "hooked" beyond help. Thanks to the encouragement of these people your needs grow faster than you are able to satisfy them. Soon you become a slave to the persons, things, and devices that tease, gratify, and promote your cravings. Your whole way of life revolves around the pursuit of pleasure and the frustration of never being able to get quite enough of it becomes an integral part of the pleasure-seeking pattern.

Whenever you deal with your pain in an egocentric way, to promote in yourself an unearned feeling of righteousness, you create a new pain, and the new pain becomes still another stimulus to craving. So you gradually become addicted to whatever it is you have used to cope with a pain that should never have existed—and *could not* have existed if you were whole within yourself. Since it does, inasmuch as most of us have never known real self-discipline, you reach for comforts to make your painful existence bearable. When any of these comforts, or crutches, which you equate with pleasure and happiness, become a way of life for you, you find it impossible to see anything wrong with them. The idea that there could be anything wrong with something you need so badly is inconceivable to you.

From the beginning, none of us have had any real love or guidance but have been tempted and pressured into living unwisely and ambitiously on an emotional basis, like animals. The pain that being thus separated from reason produces in us is a pain that should never have existed. We feel it as tension, anxiety, guilt, fear—all of which are conditions requiring treatment. But how much better the *treat* would be; i.e., instruction in how to "turn on" inside without drugs and to get right in a right way. But once we have been turned on by pressure, we cannot turn ourselves off without some counter-pressure to bring us to a state of "pleasure rest." Then, when we come to "rest," we experience conflict because of the way we went about getting there and we are powerless to do anything about it. We are at "rest" and we lack sufficient control over ourselves to turn on when we see fit. In order to get turned on again we must turn to the drug or excitement that we have come to depend on for motivation. Then, when we can no longer stand the pain of being turned on, we must turn to whatever we have come to depend on to turn us off. In other words, the controls that should exist within ourselves and belong to us are now being wielded by something outside ourselves.

As you can see from the foregoing, all our addictions point to a failing that our ego does not want to face up to. Through drugs we seek to escape the reality of our plight and inasmuch as the escape itself is another conditioning all that we manage to "escape" is the awareness of our conditioning. The image and opinion of ourselves come to rest on our escapes, and we become more wrong as the result of our many "remedies." The original weakness that started us on our escape still causes us to react wrongly under pressure but we are no longer aware of it, thanks to the pleasure conditioning we have come to depend on.

As we fail (and we surely will), we always call to mind the release or relief of both physical and mental pain that our "device" (opiate, excitement, whatever) has given us. Every pleasure or remedy becomes another problem because the more we depend on it, the farther away we get from our real problem. At the same time, the problem posed by the remedy becomes more apparent than the original problem, so if we see that we have a problem at all we prefer to believe that the remedy we are presently hung-up on is the real problem. At least it is a distraction from the more unbearable problem of our soul's failing. Now the danger of dealing with the surface problem is that (1) the more we fight it, the worse it gets—so we finally give in to it, feeling noble about the valiant fight we have put up against it; and (2) we usually swap one crutch for another. We falsely believe that we have triumphed over our problem when we have merely substituted another one for it.

So we are constantly exchanging and reshuffling our hang-ups. We cannot overcome any of them because we are always in need of something to free us from the pain of conscience and stifle our body's aches. If we give up one crutch we will take up another; or sometimes we content ourselves with a full-time fight against the present hang-up in order to avoid the danger of acquiring another. To us, the drink or the drug or the cigarette is the problem. A lifelong struggle against it endows us with the idea that we are nobly fighting evil. We are convinced of our rightness and sincerity. But all the while we are growing less effective, both at home and at work. Our problem, or the "coping" with it, takes all our strength. If we give in to it, we convince ourselves that we are finally being completely honest with ourselves—"after all, I tried"—and if we stay away from it we feel unnatural and falsely guilty for deserting it. So we conclude that our hang-ups are God-given and therefore right.

We must take a good look at our needfulness. Our economy is based upon it, of course, which is to say that our economy is based on a lie. The tradition of freedom we have inherited from our culture tells us that freedom gives us the right to be ambitious—and that is another lie.

Man's only aim should be to discover the meaning of his existence, the purpose of his being, rather than to live for power, prestige, profit, or glory. The enlightened and self-controlled man may very well be industrious, busy in a healthful and unselfish way, but he is never ambitious. When a man's ego gives in to the temptation to put what he wants ahead of what should be, he reverses the natural order.

When we reach out for what we want we fall to temptation; we become wrong. Then, we don't want to see that wrong. So we reach out for something that will help us to feel right in our wrong—and more temptation is always right there, waiting for us.

Temptation never sleeps. And when you give in to it you lose ground within yourself. The source of your conditioning shifts from the inside to the outside. Your motivation and self-image become dependent on external supports. For example, if you are tempted to make the possession of money your number one goal in life, you are wrong for putting money before principle. Of course, money can buy a better image for us—also, the "right friends"—and can make everything seem right for a while. When we get our hands on it we can argue with our conscience from our "catbird seat" and almost prove to ourselves that we are all right, just because we are so filthy rich. But a "right" that is based on money and whatever it can buy (including people) is another lie we tell ourselves, another conditioning dependency. Your need for money grows and can never be satisfied, in spite of the fact that it eventually loses its power to make you feel good. The struggle for it becomes a self-defeating process as you seek the experiences money can buy in order to maintain and heighten your sense of righteousness and importance. And the higher you reach, the lower you fall.

Your use of money to build up your image is symbolic of your rejection of your true self; but it is the rejection of your true self alone that produces the guilt. Were you to stop spending money on liquor and cigarettes, the truth of what you really are would begin to be apparent to you. But, as an egotist, you resent anything that erodes the image you have so carefully built up for yourself and your resentment turns into open war against your true self, though you do try to see yourself as Truth Incarnate with the help of your various comforts and pacifiers, including the good opinion of the people around you who respect, and may even share in, your opulence.

Fortunately, there comes a time when you can no longer fight off your incriminating conscience. I mean, we can become so wrong and guilty inside that we can't lift a finger to do a single other thing to lift our spirits. It is then that we feel the presence of reason (conscience) rising like a sun over our darkness, bursting all our illusions, rationalizations, false hopes—changing our dreams of glory into nightmares and drying up the wells of our former "happiness." Naturally, we hate that intruder (conscience, remember) with a passion. But when we start hating our true selves the sense of judgment we inflict on ourselves grows to such unbearable proportions that the only relief we can envision ahead of us is death.

When we "lose our cool," or get hung-up on something, our need for pleasure grows to take precedence over our love for the people closest to us, our family. We become involved with all kinds of intrigue and the bitterness of our reactions adds to the tension. People who encourage our ambitions and gratify our needs are really bad for us but we do not see this until they have taken us for all we have. Or until they lose their power to make us feel good and our displeasure with them unhooks us long enough for us to see that they have actually hurt us by befriending us. Then, we hate them and our hatred makes us worse. We go off licking our wounds, smarting from our bitter experience, and riding for another fall—through our next pleasure experience with someone or something we appoint to make us feel good.

When you burn your finger it feels bad. When you then plunge it into ice water it feels good. But if you had not burned it you would not be conscious of it as having any feeling at all. It would simply feel neutral and normal, like a workable part of your body. When we apply this analogy to our whole being we see that when we are upset, emotionalized by the various pressures that bombard us all, we react—either against the pressures or in favor of them. Either way we fall outside our rational processes and get "burned." Then, while we soothe our burned psyche with the artificial means we think of as happiness-producing we are defeating the natural process of recovery that would overtake us if we could learn to stand still and wait for it. If we could admit to having made a mistake and learn to bear the lesson of the pain we might become better people—even as the result of one single experience properly met. But we don't learn from experience because we are so busy escaping its lesson, plunging our burnt psyches into cold water for the instant relief that we associate with happiness—the relief that makes us think we are all right.

We seek pleasure to ease a pain that should never have existed. The pleasure, by removing the pain, removes the evidence of our ego's folly; so anything that makes us feel good gives us the impression that we are all right as a person. Thus, pleasure substitutes for the process that would lead us to real spiritual joy. Joy arises from standing firm in the faith, not being tempted or upset from our center of dignity and reason.

Conscience tells us that we are wrong when we deviate from reason, but because we are willful and pleasure-bent, we resent our spoilsport conscience and start to carry on a tug-of-war within ourselves.

Much as we want to, we cannot completely escape the inhibiting effects of conscience, so we need a little extra temptation from outside, another "remedy" to soothe the pain of our failing and enable us to forget our transgression. Lulled into a false sense of security (we call it reality) by our remedies, we step further outside the bounds of reason and we burn again. Pleasure is an escape, both from the pain and the knowledge of our failing—even a kind of reward for falling in the direction of our evil desires. Pleasure, then, can be experienced only as a contrast to pain, and we are forced to tempt other people to serve as the pleasure we need to assuage our physical needs. Of course, we need to counteract our dangerous physical needs. And of course, we need a wrong person to serve us in this way—either one who is already wrong or one we can make wrong for the purpose. And that person must be unprincipled. The pleasure he, or she, gives us will produce more pain and thus force us to embrace him, or her, again for more of the relief of pain that we call "pleasure." The pleasure actually has its own built-in pain that calls out for more pleasure—a vicious cycle.

Needless to say, inasmuch as pleasure is an escape from reality it is wrong and it is productive of pain in the end. Whatever private means of escape we use, from self-abuse (masturbation) to drug-abuse, we wind up with a bigger pain than the one we started with and it will call for bigger and better relief, until we drop dead of our excesses.

11

Drugs: the Penultimate Comforter
(Just Before Death)

<hr>

Misery loves company, and there's nothing a "wrong" person likes better than making you just as wrong as he is. "How can you know what anything tastes like until you try it?" they wheedle with serpent-like sophistry. (If you are an addict and have subscribed to this kind of argument, let's see how you react to it from the receiving end. Using the same logic, we suggest that you try the tape, "How Your Mind Can Keep You Well." After all, how can you know whether or not it works until you have tried it? You won't try it, of course, because it promises to waken you to Reality, and you'd rather remain asleep with your illusions.)

The answer to any rhetorical question is quite simple in that no intelligent person's thinking has to depend on experimentally-proven knowledge. Any reasonable person knows that he does not have to jump off a cliff to discover he can't fly, and he does not have to sample the poison to discover that it can kill him. What recourse do we have once we're dead? We can't even shout, "I've got the proof I need!" So don't be taken in by rhetorical tricks such as inept analogies and examples that have no application to the realities of the case at hand, for once you have joined the ranks of the acid-heads you will find it difficult, if not impossible, to get away from them and their destructive way of life.

While you still can, take a good look at the way they are going and ask yourself if that's the way any reasonable person should want to go. The sincerity of your motivation is the key that unlocks the technology of self-control, so that what you know is right and reasonable becomes the cogent force impelling your mind and body.

There are just two kinds of experience: inner and outer. When you don't want to face the inner truth about yourself you are forced to escape into some outer experience that will tell you you're all right just the way you are and will approve of the way you are going. Your hope is to get away from yourself, to adopt a pseudo-objective stance outside yourself where you can experience the subtle nuances of "Reality" that can be revealed only to the user of whatever it is you pin your hopes on—at least, that is what you have been led to believe. You hope in this way to arrive at a greater sensitivity to, and compassion for, your fellow men, a greater insight into the way they think and feel. Sounds marvelous, doesn't it? At first glance it seems to be all that any seeker can ask of life itself, for the ultimate goal of a seeker is to find Reality, to transcend the limitations of his own body and know the freedom from error that can be found in perfect understanding.

But you are being beguiled by the twinkle in the eyes of the serpent. Drug-induced compassion is not true compassion and drug-induced sensitivity is not the kind of sensitivity to reality that is good for us. The reality of the falsely pious is not the reality of the sincere seeker of truth. The "reality" of the drug-invaded person is the illusion that he is without fault or blemish, invincible. He is serene in an egotism that is unmarred by any self-incriminating awareness of his vanity and selfishness. Compassion to him is the understanding that every human ego need is right and proper to the ego holding it, and he develops such a remarkable sympathy for the craven needs of others that they actually think he "loves" them!

Once we are completely confused and lost we are hooked to our guides for the knowledge of God, or Truth, as we would like to know it. There are two kinds of understanding in the world. The devil, for instance, exhibits understanding for your selfishness. You might feel warmly disposed toward him out of appreciation for his concern with your desires. All the tempters—con men, promoters, pushers—do consider our needs very carefully, but is it true compassion that makes them urge us to use and lean ever more heavily on the products they have to sell us? Do they have a real interest in you or is their interest based strictly on what they consider to be their own best interest? As long as we dream ambitiously and selfishly, but lack the opportunity or motivation to obtain the stuff our dreams are made of, we look on these people as "good" for holding out a helping hand and consoling us in times of need—when we should better be looking back over the long way we've fallen in order to come to rest on such shoddy supports.

So much for the "compassion" that is not compassion. Let's look at the other claim, the one concerning the drug's ability to transport the user outside himself to a place where he can experience subtle nuances of reality that he never knew existed, which will render him more sensitive to other people. True, on occasion, the drug does momentarily clear the conscious mind of the emotional debris that is usually clogging it. A chemical reaction takes place that enables the consciousness to float up to the observation tower of pure consciousness for a short time. A small drink will often produce the same effect in us. For a moment we experience a sense of freedom and a clarity of vision that seem to be based on a groundwork of non-involvement. We may even "see" the "spirit" that is misguiding us through life's bad experiences, up to and including the drug experience. Thus, we may see "God" or mistake what we are seeing mystically *for* God—and wind up gazing in horror at the devil himself. This experience is what we call a bad trip.

A drink often has a clearing effect on the mind, but the person who is dependent on a drink for this effect is not able to handle what he sees, so he only becomes more upset than he was before. He drinks to clear his mind and what he then sees clearly inspires so much resentment and fear in him that he has to continue drinking until everything gets comfortably fuzzy again. Of course, drugs can produce the same effect.

There exists, of course, a *real* detachment, one that is not created or supported by drugs of any kind. It is the detachment that follows our conscious embrace of the presence within us that we know as "conscience." Only a sincere heart, a true seeker, is capable of the embrace that lifts us to the higher levels of our own consciousness and enables us to see by the light of reality. In that light we experience an infusion of life that precludes our being able to develop a need for drugs or any other artificial catalyst. The true desire of the seeker calls mystically for the indwelling strength that is available to every person when he is ready to avail himself of it. Drugs, on the other hand, offer an escape from the inner self to the ego that cannot bear to face the truth. The proud ego seems to be forewarned that the first truth it would see by the light of reality would be the truth that outlines our folly and exposes our past failings to our own eyes. The proud egotist shrinks from seeing that all his escapes have been engineered by the high priest of outer, environmental evil and his apostles of the dark light.

The shock of contact with the inner self produces a subtle chemical change in the body and leaves behind in us something that we come to know as fulfillment. On the surface, the effect is similar to the drug experience, but it is actually quite different in that it is not dependent upon a drug or synthetic, but upon a genuine inner experience that clears the mind and enables us to deal with problems correctly, with the courage of our own convictions and character. This inner experience not only clears your mind but it calms and stabilizes your emotions. You see immediately that in order to function as a human being you must not allow yourself to be tempted to do what is unwise in the light of reason or to become upset. In time, the simple knowing of this truth gives it authority in your life—you discover that you are actually meeting stress without becoming upset and that not being upset is a joy and that this calm joy enables you to deal effectively with all kinds of pressure. (People who deal in corruption always tell you that it's right to be emotional and ambitious, because when you are emotional and ambitious you are easy prey for them.)

The user of drugs claims to experience reality, but if his claim were true he would then be released from the need for drug experiences. The true experience of reality within himself would imbue him with all he needs as a self-contained person. If a man needs drugs to know reality, what kind of man *is* he? God preserve us from the "reality" that makes itself available to us only through a drug!

The real religious experience leaves something of its identity in us after the experience, in the form of a fullness, contentment, a change of character. We are confident in the knowledge that we can enter into that experience again, dependent upon nothing but that "something within" to turn us on. But the turn-on that drugs provide makes us dependent on drugs for the continuation of our blissful state. The incorrigible user will fight to defend the false principles upon which he stands. Just as the righteous die for what is right, the fool dies for his self-righteousness and sacrifices himself to the hideous forces that cheer him on.

Again, I see the serpent's beady eyes twinkle as he points to the fact that some users get to the point where they no longer need drugs—true in many cases. Many people claim that, having experienced reality through the drug, they have developed a new awareness and sensitivity to the needs of others. What you do not see is the quality of this sensitivity. That is, they have seen the truth about themselves and others by Truth's light, but they have not committed themselves to Truth as the overshadowing principle in their lives. They have hardened themselves to the light so that what they see so clearly doesn't bother them any more. On the contrary, they are exhilarated and excited by the blindness and the needs of others. They say to themselves, "Look at all those people who will bow down and worship us. All we have to do is 'understand' their pitiful strivings, give them what they want, and watch them grow weaker and weaker as a result of our failure to correct them. Why not? That's the way to gain a following, glory, power, profit." The manipulators didn't understand these things until they experienced an expansion of consciousness as a result of the drug. They were fools with the rest of them, but now they know and "understand" human weaknesses in a new way. Suddenly they have power and they can stay high on the excitement of that power without having to resort to drugs any more at all. Just so, a person can be a dry drunk, high on the illusion of importance he derives from helping other drunks with their drinking problem.

Let me point out here that social workers, politicians, psychologists, policemen, and reformers of all kinds fall into this category and can therefore never really help anyone. Some of their victims rebel and get worse because they see through the charade but don't know how to cope with it in an unemotional way. Others, the ones who are "saved," become the dry drunks of society, the spawning ground for future generations of social problems.

To get back to drugs, the drug experience can be so shocking to the body that the mind does "feel" itself to be objective and momentarily centered somewhere outside the body, but this condition is not one of true objectivity. The information the mind gleans here is not the kind that touches the heart in an idealistic way, but a bizarre kind, frightening to watch as it discovers its evil power to deceive the unwary. It is the ultimate in deception and self-deception. It thrives on fear and blind hope, but it is frightened to death when it meets an honest man.

Drugs, then, can be used to release the conscious mind from its emotional bonds. But a conscious mind that has not found reality can expand as a gas expands on leaking out of a confined space. The egocentric consciousness seems to expand to fill all eternity with its awareness. It experiences the "reality of oneness"— namely, that *we* are all that is—and this omnipotent confirmation of what we have always suspected swells our head in such a way that the concept of a truly higher good cannot enter. We feel secure in being the only awareness in the universe and for a moment we seem to reach out and touch everything that exists. Everything in the world is us, and we are it. We feel that we are God or that we have at least contacted Him. We feel so important, right, and omnipotent that we think we are invulnerable. We will even do dangerous things to prove the point. Some people experience such a surge of guiltlessness that they are moved to demonstrate it by stripping themselves naked and parading down the street, clothed only in what they think of as their "guileless innocence."

On the other hand, we may take just enough drug to see things clearing in perspective and the sheer horror of what we see going on in our minds is more than we can take at one time, so we may have to take a larger dose to "blow" it out. This is a bad trip and it can literally scare us to death.

This, then, is one kind of reality the user experiences: a sense of freedom, of *being* reality, even of being God. He may come back from his trip excited by his newfound belief that there is no absolute, that he is therefore free to strip himself of all inhibition of conscience and do anything at all without remorse. (He even fails to see the inherent contradiction in his absolute statement that there is no absolute.) This is the kind of reality that is the hope of all vain souls everywhere. But many can not maintain this false and limited viewpoint without drugs to enhance their feeling of power and omnipotence. And what kind of "god" is it that needs the support of drugs?

The drug experience is definitely an experience, but a deadly one indeed. It is an experience that the user defends dearly, along with all his other weaknesses and vices, for it is the penultimate comforter, the last one his body will know before death puts an end to his mortal existence. It is the escape from the knowledge of his failings, the goal of ghouls everywhere, the experience that blows the pride up like a parade balloon and leads the soul to its utter damnation. All experiences that build up our pride obligate us to the builder.

Every dictator, tyrant, tempter, or beguiler who has ever lived has succeeded only insofar as he has been able to appeal to the pride of man and keep it blind to the truth about itself and its weaknesses. He has had to know that his victims would defend every false answer and would love and defend him in gratitude for every false answer he has provided for their foolish pride to feast upon. When the ego is excited it expands until we feel that our awareness has grown to fill and encompass the universe, thus putting us solely in charge. Others then become objects—creatures we can use and abuse as we will—to serve our desires.

In order to overcome any hang-up we must first understand the nature of pride, and the way it reaches out for emotion to help it forget the pain of being proud. Have you noticed that you have made all your mistakes in moments of excitement, as when you were angry, reacting to pressure, or simply keyed up by the prospect of gain? If you have, you will see that a technology of self-control can be valuable to you. You will see how it can help you to gain mastery over the dehumanizing forces that are presently working on you. With a little technology and a sincere hunger for truth, you can learn to see clearly with nothing to aid you beyond your own judgment, a judgment that will be unclouded by prejudice and rationale, excuses and emotions. This technology is available to you at the Foundation of Human Understanding in other books and on tapes.

Teach a person to stand firm under pressure, to overcome his anger, fear, and emotional response to antagonism, and you will have a whole man who needs nothing to reassure him of his virtue or rightness because he will already *be* virtuous and right. You will have a man who can be reasoned with because he has already accepted reason as a cogent force to guide him. But when a man lacks self-control, reason cannot prevail in his life. He falls subject to rationale and to those who know how to control him by means of it. Eventually, when he sees any kind of reason as a threat to his sensitive pride, he will become a totally unreasoning beast, and nothing will be able to control him.

All of us feel secretly guilty and anxious because of our pride. We all hate our inferiority to reason. But while one Truth seeker seeks the real experience with the truth in order to overcome his pride (or perhaps to *be* overcome by true humility), another seeks only to know the kind of "truth" that will make him feel infallible and divine. Such a person is drawn to the drug experience. And even lost seekers of the true religious experience may get caught in the trap, believing that the drug can lead them to the truth they seek. Once caught and conditioned to need drugs, they find it difficult, if not impossible, to escape. They become dependent on the drugs even though they may be aware of their failing. Their dependency becomes a physical one, an evolutionary adaptation to the environment that caused the change.

Once we have fallen to the drug experience, we will defend it and evangelize it, as one who has developed an improved understanding of life as a result of that experience. We find it easy to defend our addictions because of our physical craving for the new life support they provide us. We fail to notice that our foot is resting on a lower rung of the ladder than it did formerly. And we explain our craving as "only natural." (At this point, let me remind you that "drugs" are not necessarily physical substances—a passionate lover or a chanter of meaningless gibberish can be as thoroughly "drugged" as the substance abuser, though his chances for recovery are somewhat better, thanks to the less direct assault on the physical body itself.)

As I have already pointed out, the champion of drugs is able to stop competing with his fellow egotists in the pit when he gains insight into the fact that all men are "one" in their desire to experience supreme self-righteousness. Now he becomes "compassionate" toward his fellow man's needs and leads his fellow travelers with what appears to be love and consideration; but by now he is the devil's advocate.

He no longer has to fight the common man for advantage and glory because he now sees himself as the uncommon man with power to lift others up. Now, as the high priest, he is able to maintain a sense of extreme awareness (though evil) and preserve his illusion of uniqueness, in distinct contrast to the pathetic struggle of the followers he has excited with dreams of power and advantage. The high priest, of course, never really gives his followers the key to what it is that enables him to maintain his "high" without drugs; instead, he purposely causes the others to stumble, lest they accidentally discover his secret. He finds enough excitement—profit, too—in his role of high priest to keep him madly high forever. He is free of the drug now, but who needs the drug? He is high on people instead. He has bridged the gap from contesting with others for glory to helping them to find it (just as though they could). Of course, he will not lead them too quickly to this state that he secretly and jealously believes to belong rightfully to himself alone. But he knows that others hunger to experience it, too, and this insight forms the extent of his "compassion." It is also his "understanding," his power, and his security.

Encouraged by the homage of his followers, the high priest's ego bursts into full bloom. He may even feel confident enough to declare openly that he is a god—or the devil incarnate. He knows that there *are* those who regard the devil as a god and they will be happy to identify with him. Occasionally—laugh if you will—a sudden sweep of the light of Reality can enable any of us to see Satan himself; and if the Godhead all egos aspire to still seems beyond your own grasp, you may well see your identity with Satan and express yourself accordingly.

When we start to experiment with consciousness we might go through some of the following stages:

1) We may believe that we are God.

2) We may know that there is a God, but become terrified when we discover that we are not He. Or we may become obsessed with the guilt we experience as the result of not being able to live as we should.

3) We may see Satan and assume his identity *in toto*. At first, we see that we are in error, but later we may feel challenged to identify with the error for the sake of our tender pride. A sincere man is grateful for correction, for being warned away from the trap he was about to fall into, but the incorrigibly egotistical man feels threatened by your admonition. Why? Because he has become—he is—the mistake you are alluding to. He has identified himself so completely with the wrong that when you warn him against it he takes your correction personally. He feels that you are "taking his name in vain."

The practice of hallucinating continuously in order to escape from the concept of a God greater than ourselves may not always be caused by the residual poison of a drug like LSD. It might be the result of a psychic need to escape or a need to maintain a feeling of omnipresence. This need forces us to keep the memory of past experiences alive through reminiscing or perhaps reliving an old romance. Sometimes an experience of shock can make such a profound impression on us that we can never forget the trauma that resulted from it. We are too worn out to fight the memory of that one bad experience too many, added to a lifetime of them, and so we are forced, like the person who has had a bad car accident, to live it over and over again, compulsively. It is the bad trip on the broad highway that leads to Hell.

12

The Wicked Loving Father

The following conversation has been excerpted from one of my regular radio talk show programs, tape #2261:

Caller: I am 17 and I am a senior in high school. My parents are divorced and a lot of times I feel like they are playing head games with me. My mom doesn't live here any more and I've been forced to live with my father. My mom moved out. My dad lives with me now and it's kind of like I've been forced to live with him because my mom and I don't get along together. He's got a girl friend and I get pressured by him to act certain ways around her.

RM: Of course, your father is out of order and is setting a bad example for you. And I'm sure you resent that, don't you?

Caller: Yes.

RM: Don't resent him. Just observe that this is not a proper example to set for anyone.

Caller: I do. I observe a lot of what my parents do to me.

RM: But don't resent them for it. Every inordinate form of behavior, outrageous form of behavior, immoral form of behavior, is a temptation for you to judge and hate. To survive this unjust environment you must discover the difference between discerning and judging. In other words, what I want you to do—and I want you to make a practice of this for the rest of your life—is to discern, unemotionally, your father's bad example, or anyone's for that matter, and allow resentment to pass.

Caller: He uses me to make himself feel like the father that he is not.

RM: That is the temptation. But you have an alternative. Observe calmly his wicked use of you, lest it become a temptation to judge. He may spoil you with money to buy your respect. Tell me, how does he use you?

Caller: In the past he has always said that I take and take and take, and it's true. One time when he offered me money I didn't take it—and then he resented me for that.

RM: Sure. I understand that. Because, as you see, he is trying to buy you off.

Caller: Right.

RM: By giving you money, which is a temptation, he is trying to buy respect for a very unrespectable self. Having maneuvered you into a position of weakness and need, he forces you into the humiliating role of accepting a handout that is calculated to represent your acceptance of him as a person. When you accept what you need from him it's like giving him a stamp of approval.

Caller: Right. And when I didn't accept his help he got angry.

RM: Of course, he would. His kind never gives anything without wanting something in return. So when you refused to take the money it was a sign of rejection. Rejection is very threatening to a man whose false sense of worth is dependent on being accepted. He has a natural obligation toward you, of course, because he brought you into this world and must therefore provide for you until you are able to stand on your own two feet.

Caller: My mother has completely rejected me. She forced me on him and makes him do everything for me. She resents it when I ask her to do anything for me.

RM: She won't do anything for you at all? That is probably because she had the same problem with your dad as you have. She was also an object of use. She may have a problem with helping anyone because she has experienced firsthand what it is like to be "helped."

Caller: Right.

RM: Perhaps also she is not in a financial position to help.

Caller: I know.

RM: But your father does owe it to you. I want you to listen carefully, please. Without becoming emotional. Okay? Can you hear me all right?

Caller: Yes.

RM: I want you to observe calmly what your father is and how he is buying you off. Notice how you resent him for that, and how it threatens him when you don't accept his gifts, so he resents you back. And then notice how you resent his resentment. Is that too fast for you?

Caller: No.

RM: (continuing)...and how you feel guilty for resenting his resentment, and how that guilt makes you accept money. So here you are, back in the same boat again, accepting him even more, degraded and humiliated, existing to serve his rotten pride. Resentfully, you take his handout—which is playing the game, giving him his stamp of approval. You can't say anything because you are choked up with rage and afraid of losing material security. And you have no skills, either, because he made sure you would remain dependent on him. You are becoming confused, and your energy is being drained through emotional turmoil. You can't go out and become independent because your mind isn't with it. And because you can't get away you resent that too. All you are doing is becoming more dependent on his "generosity" and giving him what he wants in exchange for what you have to have, while at the same time you hate it.

Caller: I feel obligated, like I have to make him...

RM: Happy.

Caller: Yes.

RM: If you don't, he torments you, and your own guilt for existing to serve him torments you, and your resentment torments you. The only peace you have ever known has come from giving in, bowing and scraping for money, which leads to the next torment. There is never peace for you, as you have already noticed. There is no peace in making him "happy."

Caller: But I feel like—since I've taken it, then I should try to. But I can't grow. By taking it or not taking it.

RM: Yes. In effect you are damned if you do and damned if you don't.

Caller: Yes!

RM: So let me show you a better way, where there is no shame for you either way—but where your father will feel the shame he badly needs to experience. Would you like that?

Caller: Yes, I would.

RM: Okay. Let's go back to my opening remark about learning not to resent your father for what he is doing, for the games he is playing with your head—using you to assuage his guilt so that he can always feel good about himself. Every egotist has a somebody or something he is using for this purpose. Your father, like all men, married for security; people drink and have drinking buddies who don't know they are being used; the sick swallow drugs to make themselves feel good again. People have always used one another the same way your father is using you. It is not all that unusual for parents to make children take on their guilt, even the responsibility for their sicknesses, so that—out of obligation—the child does what is required and the parent then feels happy and well. That is the only "wellness" that wicked people know. Rest assured, as part of you gets well, your dad will get sick. And don't be surprised at his outrage. He will attempt to make you feel that you are hurting him.

Caller: That's right.

RM: If you are more guilty than your father he doesn't feel so bad about himself, does he?

Caller: That's right.

RM: So this is simply a game he plays, which he is not aware of because you are becoming more guilty than he—by taking on his sin. You must give it back to him, back to where it belongs. As long as you react with resentment and judgment you can't make him aware, because your sin is all he sees. He doesn't see his own. You are both looking at each other's. When you take his "favors" all he sees is your shame—not his own. Is that correct?

Caller: Are you saying I am more guilty?

RM: You are more guilty.

Caller: Why?

RM: Because judgment makes you guilty. Resentment sustains judgment and judgment blocks the light of love, the light that might enable him to see himself.

Caller: I think a lot about the things he is doing.

RM: You think revenge. Look, you are playing the game too. You are seeking a way to make him suffer, to relieve yourself of guilt. But that only makes you more guilty. I don't intend to be mean by saying you are worse than he is, but in a sense you are. If you were not, he could never feel better about himself. Follow that?

Caller: Yes.

RM: You are deteriorating through your relationship with him. And you are conscious of being degraded, but he is not. That's the problem. You are more sensitive. You could end up in a mental hospital one of these days with a nervous breakdown. And then you might see him as a dutiful father, an angel from heaven coming to the rescue, spending his money and getting the best doctors—all the while driving you more crazy through your hatred of being forced to accept the same old phony help. Is that correct?

Caller: I've tried to kill myself before.

RM: I don't doubt you have. He has got you coming and going. He possesses you as an object of use, degrading your soul for a bizarre sense of well-being. You must find the secret way to keep yourself from being destroyed. Are you meditating?

Caller: No.

RM: Then you should get my meditation materials. Because the secret way is through learning how to become objective. You can not learn that just by listening to my radio advice. You need the cassettes and if you can't afford the suggested price I will send them to you without charge. So be sure to call after the program and give your name and address.

Caller: Okay.

RM: You need to learn how to be calm with your father, no matter what dirty tricks he pulls. And then if he becomes angry with you for whatever stand you take, you won't just reflect his mood in the old "monkey-see-monkey-do" way. You will find the power within to deal with the power without. When he sees that he can't move you to the right or to the left, either by being super nice or super cruel—when he sees you won't fall for that, he will know his game is up!

Caller: I got in trouble at school one day for talking and he came home from lunch and wrote me a nasty note and put it on my door for me to see when I got home. And then another day I get an A on a test and he's showering me with "Oh, how proud I am of you!"

RM: That's the game of praise and condemnation, designed to throw you off balance. But you see, those two extremes are designed to take away your awareness so that you can never observe him with a calm mind—with a perceptive, discerning, non-judgmental look. All guilty people are terrified of being *observed, perceived.* Your father senses that danger. He feels that you are "up to something" when you refuse to take his money. That is why he becomes angry. He knows you will reflect his anger. Your resentment will put out the light. It will make you guilty and cause you to make up to him shamefully by doing what he wants you to do. He makes you guilty whether you grovel in the dirt of appreciation resentfully or refuse his offering out of anger and pride. He is afraid of being observed, and he is afraid of innocence. He doesn't mind if you love/hate him because either emotion works to his advantage.

Caller: And I shouldn't be doing that.

RM: I want you to observe him without adding that flash of resentment. That is to say, watch as from a distance. Let the flash of resentment pass. Do you understand? Let me hear you say it.

Caller: Okay, I can understand...observe what he's doing...

RM: Without getting upset over it. Watch the upset in yourself and make sure to watch it long enough to see it go away. Otherwise, the guilt of resentment will stain your observation and cause you to doubt what you see and become afraid. Add to resentment the guilt of doubting yourself and you have the ingredients for making up to your father, easing the pain you feel by easing the guilt he feels. You see, you are doing the same thing he is: seeking approval for something rotten in yourself. You can't see it now because you are too busy judging him. If you want to stop playing the game and being used, then stop hating him. Then you won't need to love him or need him to love you. I am telling you to give up resentment.

Caller: Is that the point where you let go?

RM: That's the point where he loses all control over you.

Caller: Right.

RM: And at the point of innocence, you can accept his money or not. You can't go wrong. Right now, what can you do? You're his daughter. You must be able to accept his food and shelter without feeling guilty, simply because you realize it's his duty toward you. If you can resist resenting the shabby way he discharges his duty, you can not be made to feel guilty for taking what is right for you to have. You can, if you wish, refuse his help at the appropriate time and not feel guilty. Depending on the circumstances, you will be in total control. When you hold your peace inside and when you no longer fall for that "good-guy bad-guy" routine—when you remain in your center—that's when grace shines in you. And then the guilty no longer see *you*. They see the spirit of God in you. You will never be guilty of anything ever again and nothing you can ever do will be wrong or go wrong. Nothing. People who try to put out your light will be judged by the standard they have tried to destroy.

Caller: So I just have to observe him.

RM: *Observe him.*

Caller: But how do I know when I'm not judging?

RM: I told you: when you are not angry.

Caller: When I'm not angry?

RM: Yes. And by the way, when your father discovers he can no longer use his ordinary duty, taking care of you as a father should, to make you guilty, he may reject his natural role of protector and throw you out of the house, since you would be, in his eyes, an unappreciative good-for-nothing. Be prepared. It could happen. But again, resist the temptation to resent him and puff up with the serpent of pride. That will be the icing on your cake.

13

What Price Friends?

When I was a small boy, I remember being embarrassed by any display of affection. For some reason, the sticky emotions that were so much enjoyed by everyone else seemed strange and unattractive to me. As a result, I could not bring myself to participate in such demonstrations. I remained distant, unwilling to involve myself on an emotional level.

There was something about the whole emotional scene that alerted me to stand back and remain "on guard," even though the emotion might be one I could feel entitled to revel in as far as the people around me were concerned. Pride, for instance. I remember standing back to admire something I had made and feeling a little puff of pride as I did so, but even as I was feeling the lift of pride, I sensed on a deeper level that there was something not quite right about the charge of excitement I was feeling. I knew that I did not want to feel that way again. When emotions of anger and resentment would start to flare up, I backed away from them, too, and they slowly dissolved.

As a result, I have grown up with little fear and conflict, with none of the ugly problems that most people are prey to, thanks to my having held on to an unwavering faith in the promptings of my own conscience. Looking back, I can see that most people have been too quick to doubt what their conscience is trying to tell them and have reached instead for the glib reassurances of the world around them. "There, there, little boy, you have a perfect *right* to be angry at that big bully." Or: "What a great report card! How *proud* you must be!"

I am sure you have experienced similar moments of discomfort when you were forced to witness some emotional scene, especially if you were expected to "take sides" or participate in some way, but you probably didn't fare as well as I did. You were probably too quick to doubt yourself, to assume that those who were criticizing you or pressuring you for some emotional response were right and you were wrong about what you were observing. So you wound up doubting the truth that you had once seen so clearly and you became worldly. To this very day, you could probably trace most of the mistakes you have made, along with most of the injustices you have suffered at the hands of others, to the fact that you are still doubting your own common sense, still deferring so much to what "they" say you should be feeling that you are lost in a sea of borrowed feelings, powerless to stop the process of doubting that has torn you away from your original center of being.

What a marvelous thing it would be if you could find the way to lose faith in the false faith you have acquired—if you could wipe the slate clean—and get back to your original point of view.

Let me help you. Let me part the veil of mystery and unmask the *modus operandi* behind some of the things that you have allowed yourself to get caught up with, so that through your own enlightened understanding you can doubt the world more perfectly, for until you *see people for what they are, you will be unable to doubt the perfect doubt*. It was precisely because you doubted yourself and believed in people that you were pulled down into a world of phony emotional love, a world of frustration, disillusion, suffering, disease, and dying.

You find it easy to doubt yourself because such an easygoing attitude draws approval and acceptance from the people around you, and if you are proud—as you know you have been—you have always placed far too much importance on being liked and accepted by others. One minute you may see people exactly as they are, but a moment later you come down to accept their approval and whoosh! All is forgotten as you bask in the sunshine of their admiration. How glorious it is to be accepted just the way you are—or is it?

Let's look at the price you have paid for your stamp of approval. As the result of doubting yourself you have gone along with the crowd, laughing with them, dressing like them, and finally, sinning with them. And the more you have gone along with the crowd, the more you have had to wrestle with the anxiety that is the constant companion of guilt; but instead of seeing your anxiety and guilt as the result of having sold out to your friends, you feel it as a fear of losing the friends that you need so desperately. And as you have become prouder and guiltier, you have required your friends to be more corrupt and pretentious. You are compelled to go on doubting yourself for relief from guilt as you dig a little deeper for each new set of low-life liars to support you.

Your inherited doubt is the very doubt that led the first man toward sin in the first fall. For the rest of us, his heirs, doubting the Truth is no longer a matter of choice. It is a more compulsive thing, a secret means of relieving the ego's inherited pride, along with its inherited anxiety. The Devil himself feeds our ancient need to doubt what is right in order to go on striving pridefully.

By far the most important Truth for you to discover is the Truth concerning your origin, your heritage; for once you discover where you have been coming from, you will be able to experience a marvelous need for salvation from where you are going.

People are controlled and destroyed through their weaknesses. And the main reason they fail to see what is happening to them is that they somehow manage to think of their failings as virtues. Whenever you believe that some failing is a virtue, you enjoy being tempted to experience it more fully, equating the fuller experience with "growing up." People who excite you appear to be friends, and you follow them blindly and without question, all for the sake of the glorifying feelings they inspire in you. Their "orders" may be coming from Satan himself, but the only credential you require of them is their unquestioning acceptance of you as you are.

The occasion of your fall always slips in during one of those special moments of righteous passion: A flash of anger, perhaps, or love, which you think you feel toward people when they make you feel sorry for them, or when they excite your failings with their acceptance of your support.

Our whole society is teetering on the brink of disaster, thanks to the sanctimonious, almost dutiful, manner in which we have come to accept our craven animal needs as virtues. The animal emotions you feel are those that rise as your soul descends. You come down to experience emotion whenever your ego fails to do what is right or when it reacts in a wrong way to stress. At the same time, the pride that you cling to for the notion of your infallibility can neither see nor accept the evidence of your failing for what it is. Pride insists on seeing the animal feelings that greet the ego's fall as something uniquely human and divine, a kind of godly sensitivity unifying and validating the world. Alas, the proud one is merely sensitive *to* the world, and the evil continues to control him through his feelings.

Every time you lose yourself in feelings of animal love or anger, and you see those feelings as virtues, you are unconsciously affirming your belief in an evolutionary origin, regardless of any religious conviction you might profess to have in any other theory concerning the creation of man.

You dare not see where your troubles originate, any more than the drunkard dares to suspect his friend, the bottle, as the source of his. It is the nature of pride to revel in the temptations that excite a man to glory in his failings and prevent him from seeing that his real salvation depends on his knowing and accepting the real truth. After all, if you are simply an evolving creature you have nothing to worry about—just go on feeling what the other animals are feeling and you will improve naturally as evolution runs its course. The evolutionist certainly knows how to make life easy for the prideful, but how do his theories sit with you? Do you really think we are slowly evolving toward perfection, or do you agree with me that we have fallen from our former state of purity and innocence as children of God?

Let's look at some of the messes we can get into as the result of giving in to our feelings:

You feel pressure from people, so you yield to their demands. Now, instead of feeling pain and uncertainty, you feel a surge of relief and acceptance. Don't you see that when you give service or engage in some generous act as the result of having been pressured, you are being "loved" or rewarded for your weakness. Of course, falling under another person's control for the sake of being accepted does feel like "falling in love." Falling, yes. Love, no.

People who give in to avoid arguments tend to love and to serve out of a need to be admired for their dependability and goodness—weakness, really. When you yield to a person's unbearable pressure you may find yourself compelled to serve someone you think you love, but actually hate. Any person that you think you love is always your enemy; if he is not already, give him time—he will be. As long as your ego refuses to see its compulsiveness you will look on your feelings as the real thing, genuine "love." Every knight in shining armor knows how to control you and make you adore him for his "charms," which are nothing more than a well-honed ability to manipulate you through your feeling reactions. He may look like a lover, but he is an enemy. Think about it.

You grew up under pressure and somewhere down the line you have yielded to it; so your pressure source has rewarded you with praise and called you "good. " Of course, you have taken that person's praise as an expression of real "love." As a result, you are now conditioned to need the kind of love that is your reward for being weak and unable to resist pressure. Forevermore, unless you wake up, you are conditioned to surrender to pressure in order to sustain the notion of your own goodness that you "bought" from the original source of pressure in your life.

No doubt you are friendly and likable enough, a devoted son or daughter or husband, father, mother, or wife; yet you are secretly unhappy, and you don't even realize that your sense of wrongness about the way you are living is the direct result of your having been conditioned to find ego satisfaction and "virtue" in the weakness that pretentious people just "love" to use for their own advantage. As far as anyone can see, you display all the usual devotions of a God-fearing individual, but you are allowing yourself, compulsively, to be used by all the wrong people and all the wrong causes. They know what is going on, but you don't. At various times, you may have sensed that there was something wrong with your relationships, but you cured your uneasiness by bending over backward to please others, giving of yourself to the last drop.

You have become dependent upon pressure; without it, you cannot function, nor can you keep yourself assured of your goodness. So, even when pressure is lacking, you find yourself serving everyone around you with alacrity, just as though the pressure were there. Eventually, you involve the innocent by converting them into a source of pressure also. Although they had no intention of manipulating you, you make of yourself such a juicy morsel, so ripe for the plucking, that you lead them into temptation. Of course, when things get to the point that you see you are being used, it won't occur to you to realize that you are the guilty one, and by that time, thanks to your blandishments, the users may not be so innocent any more either. You not only serve those who already know how to take advantage of you, but you set up the innocent to take the same kind of liberties.

The meanest, most conniving people in the world can bet their life on their ability to buy your loyalty. All they have to do to get what they want from you is to turn you on with the kind of pressure that helps you to discover your godlike generosity and goodness.

As you become thoroughly conditioned to surrender for the sake of ego acceptance, you tend to look to certain kinds of people who represent the kinds of pressure you have been corrupted to need. All they have to do is resemble someone who was familiar to you during childhood—then, without realizing you are doing so, you unleash the energy of your old secret resentments in a great flood of kindness. Have you noticed that even the phantoms flitting in and out of your mind are clothed in the familiar forms of loved ones and they compel you to serve their devilish demands?

Evil, then, is what you really love; you are enslaved to it all your life for the sake of the image of yourself you need to cling to. You must see in your associations the familiar shadow of the original evil, the one that corrupted you; otherwise, you will find yourself unable to function as the world's most wonderful human being. You may even go so far as to spoil your own children, drawing up through them the guileful spirit you need to turn you on to your own greatness. An ambitious man will shower his wife with gifts in order to turn her into the rotten, spoiled, nagging witch that his mother was. He "loves" better that way. He also grows more ambitious.

The good image you have of yourself has grown from weakness, from yielding to pressures. And your weak goodness grew from the seeds of deeply buried resentments. First, you yield to another's demand almost casually, in order to avoid recognizing a gut-level pulling that signifies your inherited enslavement to the sin authority. When it dawns on you that you might have done better to resist, you become resentful in order to find the energy to do so, but you finally give in to relieve the pain caused by your resentment. In the moment of your acceptance you see your oppressor suddenly transformed into a friend, almost an "angel of light," and the problem of your compulsion seems to disappear as though touched by a magic wand.

But your troubles have only just begun. From this point onward you will be unable to live your own life. People start taking advantage of your "goodness," and you burn with a resentment that backfires into a stronger desire to please. With a slight twist of logic you can turn things around to make it appear that you have the power to make bad people into good ones by the way you answer to their cries. You feel like God with his children.

Being God now makes you shoulder the full responsibility for everyone's well-being. Being all things to all people, you give your all. Everyone runs you ragged and drains the life out of you. Depression sets in, and you begin to resent everyone for the pressure you feel bearing down on you and forcing you to prove yourself over and over again, forcing you to gargantuan feats of kindness and devotion to these lesser gods in a desperate attempt to make them acknowledge you, until you just can't rise to the occasion another minute. When you see that you are not getting the approval you need to assuage your anxiety, you head straight for the classic nervous breakdown. You think that others drove you to it with their pressures, but the unbearable guilt you feel is your own conscience at work.

While resentment of others can help you forget your own wrongs, it can also give you the motivation you need in order to be "good" again, perhaps this time toward those you have been neglecting. As a professional people pleaser, you are devoted to many wrong purposes and false gods, proudly trying to compensate for feelings you cannot understand. You come back home from one of your volunteer efforts, and out of the pressure of guilt you serve the family you have been neglecting. Whether it's your family or the outside source of pressure, you follow the same pattern. You resent people for making you feel guilty and the guilt of resenting them drives you to exude a "kindness" whose hidden mainspring is hate.

What you are guilty of, more than anything else, is the attitude that views all your surrenders as acts of love. If you are inclined to see your failings as virtues, you will be obliged to go on serving people mindlessly and endlessly. People often prefer death to facing the truth about themselves, so they commit suicide before the agony of reality can catch up with them. Then there are the multitudes who kill themselves to end the agony of their compulsive obeisance to an evil god.

Why must we cling so to our compulsions and come to such a wretched end? How does it all start?

It is resentment that triggers your first ungracious resistance to any pull or obligation. You feel the natural gut-level pull to oblige the sinner in your life who outranks you, after all, but instead of letting yourself realize your lower-level weakness, you feel resentment welling up to help you rise above the command. Because resentment happens to be a prideful response to temptation, you experience the growth of your ego as a painful conflict, an inner pressure. And then you resent the pressure. But your ego escapes the realization of its own guilt by ascribing the "unjust" pressure to some outer source.

Resentment-based judgment produces some fringe benefits for your ego. One of them makes you feel superior to the wicked person who is, or seems to be, the source of the pressure; also, you seem to be kinder than your oppressor, at least in your own eyes. Although we are all born subject to the indwelling spirit of evil in those who came into the world before us, and they are our superior officers in the order of hell by virtue of seniority if nothing else, our pride can not acknowledge obedience to anything. It never could. So, thanks to our pride and the foolish ways in which we try to resist being put down, we remain slaves to sin.

The oppressor understands your secret dilemma. He knows that he need only assert himself in order to make your resentment of him backfire on yourself and change into the guilt that will cause you to play into his hands. Once you capitulate, you no longer see demand as demand or resentment as resentment. All you see now are your "virtues": love, longsufferance, loyalty, justice, and mercy. You are going to outshine him if it takes every ounce of your martyrdom to do so. Just as you are able to feel superior to those you hate, so also can you see yourself as superior to those you serve. Your mind turns everything around, so that it is not you who is doing the service, but they who are serving your need to give of yourself, even as God gives, to the strong and the weak alike. So you go through life *making* friends, *making* bad people into good ones, *making* everything and everyone serve your ego. Whether they like it or not, they all fall in line and play their parts—until someone manages to rebel and take his stand as your real honest-to-goodness enemy.

Having been set up to be a weak/good person from childhood, you remain a good Joe all your life, gravitating to those people in whom you can detect the familiar spirit of your past. It is love at first sight. But underneath all your devotions you sense stirrings of a seething resentment against loving and being loved, and an evanescent feeling of futility dances in and out of your carefully-wrought construct of a boundless love for people.

Guilt is a self-condemnation that will give you no peace until you get right with yourself. The lower you sink, the more sensitive you become to other people's needs, which are really demands in disguise. Indeed, "kind" people who have grown to use/love you really do have a need, a terrible need that can never be satisfied, no matter what you do for them. These depraved devil-possessed persons are utterly dependent on you, so accustomed have they become to being served your gut on a silver platter. So, if ever you fail to feed yourself unreservedly to them, their "love" will turn to hate, and they will withhold their approval of you until you love them into being good to you again.

Let me remind you of a vital point that I touched on earlier; namely, that you tend to react as though people were pressuring you even when they are not. When a lustful sailor stands on the street corner to watch the pretty girls go by, he construes every little sidelong glance, every toss of a lovely head as "just what the doctor ordered," just the pressure he needed to inspire in himself a kind of lustful "love" toward those he is using for their excitement value. The effect of this pressure often expresses itself as an instant liking for people, a "love-at-first-sight" involvement. It forms the basis for all the romantic, sexual love affairs that have nothing at all in common with true love. It also accounts for the mounting statistics on violence and divorce.

You have never related to people honestly. You have always rebelled, or given your all, to avoid seeing the shame of your compulsiveness. Indeed, you may feel as though you have invested something of your Divine goodness in the people you "love," and that feeling accounts for your not being able to live either with or without your mate.

You have used people to stimulate you into acts of goodness and love. You have obliged them to play a special role for you, a very wicked one indeed. As a result, you have lost part of yourself to those you have used in this way. They have become your whole life, the reason for your existence. You yearn for them and you suffer what they suffer. You feel that you can never be happy until they are happy, and to that end, you give under subtle pressure until you have nothing left to give.

Let me remind you of another vital point, which is that once a person has been corrupted to adapt to his environment, he needs that environment. He is dutiful toward it for the sake of what his ego now craves from it. I have referred to this craven need for environment as animal magnetism. Now, combine animal magnetism with your need to give in to pressure and you produce a twofold power that, to you at least, has all the earmarks of love.

Those who upset you suck you into their private hell. Haven't you noticed that irritating people have a way of getting anything they want out of you? Your natural propensity to give in to pressure, combined with your resentment, compels you with a double force.

Life could be so simple if you would just stop struggling against your inherited inferiority and admit to the fact that it is controlling you. See how your resentment and your struggles to break free have resulted in futility. Also, see how your resentment has propelled you toward the more subtle surrenders, like drinking or smoking.

It is exciting to a woman to discover how much power she has over a man when he "falls in love" with her. All she has to do to consolidate her control is play a role, a role that unfortunately turns out to be a wicked and dishonest one, but she must continue to play it for the sake of the feeling of power that she grows to need and "love." So she is obliged to go on being used and becoming more dishonest and evil in the process. In the role of temptress she finds both agony and ecstasy, the one leading inexorably to the other and back again. All men are unconsciously attracted to what is *wrong* with a woman. The wrong is what an egocentric man feels to be *right* for him. What starts with her yielding to his sexual failing proceeds to his yielding to whatever the woman demands of him and it all seems like loving until the woman turns into a witch.

The guile in the woman, which brings forth the brute in the man, soon becomes the irritant on which he bases his existence; and his ego survival, as well as hers, keeps them tied to that base.

Women have terrible conflicts because of the role they are obliged to play. They also have problems with their innate wickedness—the wickedness that men "love" so much. Men, on the other hand, have problems with their apelike weakness, the weakness that women seem to encourage so "lovingly." Women are forced to accept the brute just the way he is because of the pride they take in the man's compulsive love. Then, they turn around and spoil their children in order to create the kind of pressure they need if they are to realize their love and devotion toward them.

The woman's ego descends to encourage the beast, and the man descends to accept the devil's abiding love—all very exciting, distracting, and entertaining.

The principle of surrender as the hallmark of love lies at the very core of the meaning of love; but it signifies true love only when the surrender is to God. Unfortunately, a man may feel justified in the giving of himself to others, even the devil himself, because, in his pride, he sees himself as the God to whom he is surrendering. In his surrender, he feels that he is disseminating Divine love throughout the world. He reinforces his idea of himself as Mr. Wonderful by surrendering to the ideal of his greatness. At the same time, he seems to bring into existence a lesser god, created for the sole purpose of sustaining his identity as a god.

When you take on a god identity, you feel responsible for the whole world. People who think they need you will drain the great life out of you, and when you have nothing left to give, the shock of Truth can drive you to a nervous breakdown. Because you have this terrible need to give of yourself to everyone, you spoil people by letting them take advantage of your goodness until they can hardly function for themselves. Oh, how you love your tyrants, your helpless cripples, those larcenous brats who make such outlandish demands on you, the "great one." In your eyes, their pressure, their appeal, is the living symbol of your greatness; so, of course, you cannot resist returning their love like a God in heaven, harking to the cries of his little ones.

With each noble, humanitarian act, you are drawing into existence fat cats, tyrants, and devils, fashioned out of your

Divine gut and destined for a life of frustration and torment. The net result of all your loving is a horrible case of anxiety, simply because you are serving evil to build a glorious illusion for your ego and you are running from the light of Truth. Without realizing what you are up to, you superimpose the nature of an old childhood relationship with a pressure source—your mother, perhaps—onto a current relationship with your wife, your boss, your buddy, your close friends. In every instance, you are trying to make the new relationship serve you better than the old one ever did when you were young and helpless. Your yearning continues to tend toward the kind of relationship that corrupts you, lest you be left alone, bereft of the acclaim to which you feel entitled. You feel guilty, and for good reason.

You surrender now to escape the guilt and to avoid realizing your servitude as servitude, and the more you surrender to get rid of your guilt, the more it nips at your heels and forces you into still more compulsive behavior. You surrender also for the false sense of security you derive from seeing your failure as "love," a love that transforms you into a divine being, without fault or blame. You fill with pride in the abandonment of being that certifies you to yourself as being "whole-hearted," "true-blue," "filled with undying devotion."

The whole concept of loving and being loved is related to Supreme Goodness in our minds; but when you presume to identify yourself with that source of all Good, all hell breaks loose. Your insistence on blinding yourself to Reality in favor of the illusion drives your consciousness into a total involvement with emotion, so that you can no longer see anything as it exists objectively, in reality. Now that you have become God, you have no need to question your feelings, because if anything feels good to God, it has to be good.

Beware of the sweet, kind, and unnaturally obliging persons who impress you with their goodness by taking an instant liking to you. Anyone with the perspicacity to see what a great person you are must deserve your respect, you think, but don't let flattery suck you in. Stand back. Wait until you see what the tempter had in mind for you. If he catches you off guard, he will convert you to his use. Of course, you will be most vulnerable to this kind of attack if the tempter happens to be of the opposite sex.

Anyone who looks to temptation for his life's sustenance will first trap you into making a favorable judgment, and when you oblige him you become the support of what he is. He will draw up through your corrupted ego all the unclean things, faults, and familiar spirits he was conditioned to need at an early age. "Nice" people can change your personality completely and use it to support their craven need to play God. They can sow terrible confusion in your mind. And it all started with Adam: the need of his ego to function as his own god.

This ego need that we all inherited from Adam does not always "sit well" with you, especially when you are called upon to play the supporting role for a bigger ego. You can't understand why it gives you guilty feelings that you can't seem to get rid of except by yielding once again to the corrupter's flattery and letting him spoil you again. Then you, too, feel identified with God's goodness. So you start out as a pocket devil, but your tyrant potential may be even greater than anything known to those who first enlisted you to serve them.

The devil gave Adam the starring role by appealing to his pride, but he managed to hang onto the real power through the woman. God help you if you persist in this nonsense all the way to the ultimate surrender/acceptance experience, whose flip side gives you the illusion that you are being accepted as God coming into His own spiritual abode at last.

It could catch up with you on your death bed when the angel of death comes to take you to your "rest," or you might enter one of those living hell relationships that transforms you into an indentured zombie to some despicable tyrant. Or you might get caught up with one of those holy flower-loving "avatars" who come down to gather up the "children of God." Do you see how the false gurus, emissaries from Hell, gain the power to collect all the compulsive lovers in the full bloom of their pride?

After a lifetime of compulsions, surrenders, involvements, escapes—all edging you closer and closer to hell—your need to embrace the "loving" lord of the most low will be greater than ever—along with the illusion that you are the one in control. Now you "make" the supreme embodiment of the devil accept you at the lowest point of your descent, and the lifetime of failures and surrenders will assure you that you have arrived at ultimate perfection...and you are gone.

14

Coping With Manipulation

If someone hates you one moment and smothers you with love the next, what are his true feelings for you? Where is his integrity? Think for a moment and you will see that he has none. What kind of creature swings between moods of kindness and acceptance, cruelty and rejection? A manipulator, that's who, one who has fallen victim to manipulation himself, and as a result, is under the control of another spirit.

Manipulators can not say "no" to more powerful personalities, but they are cruel and willful in relationships with those who are weaker than they are. The victim reacts, and presto, another manipulator is born. Haven't you noticed that when you allow your nice, mannerly children to get caught up with the wrong crowd, you can hardly recognize them when they come home? When you try to correct them they put up a stubborn shield of bravado in defense of their newly-acquired wrong.

That stubborn defensiveness duplicates the original willfulness that entered the human race through the sin of pride. When you encounter it, you are not dealing with the person himself, but with a powerful will that is operating through him. And you may even be seeing a mirror image of yourself, for in one way or another we have all surrendered our self-control to some seductive authority.

When you encounter that stubborn willfulness in defense of wrong within your own family, you must deal with it in a very special way. You must not get angry when they try to provoke you. And you must not fall for their love games. You must realize that you are not dealing directly with your child, wife, or husband, but with another will that has displaced their own. They defend this will as their own, both because it has been supportive to them in a previous situation and to save face in the present encounter. They may realize that "something has come over them," and they are not "themselves," or they may not. They may have become so identified with the alien will that they are enslaved to its service, thinking that they really want to do what the alien presence urges, whether it be to steal or kill or even commit suicide.

If you don't understand what you are dealing with, it will suck you in. Your vital force will join with the awful power you sought to oppose.

In children, the ancient wish to play God translates into a craving for acceptance. This craving makes a child susceptible to pressure from his friends. Children will give their pocket money, and even their bodies, to hold on to the low-life friends who stroke their pride. These young innocents are blind, defensive, and possessive in all their relationships, but what they feel is the manipulator's will that has taken possession of them. If you are not wise to the ways of the malevolent spirit of the world, operating through your children, you can say goodbye to your chances for a serene and happy home life with your family.

Remember what I have told you about resentment: The manipulator uses it to seize control. Therefore, be very firm, but very calm—never upset—in your efforts to protect or rescue your loved ones. Watch your emotions, for you can't help but express them by your demeanor. If your child sees that you are upset, he will resent your effort to guard him and his resentment will make easier prey of him in his next encounter. You must require him to stay away from the wrong crowd, but you must do so calmly, with patience. Great power dwells in patience. Patience expresses the protective love that, not being of this world, moves a child to reflect upon who really cares for him and who does not. *Children need to experience the clarity and power that sustains them through the patience of loving parents, until they can tap its source in their own hearts.* Unless you can show them by your example the contrast between "street smarts" and the power of loving patience, they will be taken over by the spirit of the street, the crowd, the world.

What are you to do when confronted by a child, wife, husband, boss, anyone seething with emotion and spoiling for a fight? Always, the answer remains the same: Be in your center. Hold fast to the quiet place within you, lest you contribute your energy to the force that is operating through the agitated person. If you, too, become upset, you will be powerless to counteract the overshadowing spirit; as you lose ground, you will feel yourself becoming its instrument rather than its adversary. The very wrong you thought you were opposing springs to life inside yourself. Once you let it in, you can no longer say no to its influence and it will change your viewpoint. Now, as an agent of wrong rather than an agent of correction, your vacillating stance will confuse the one you were trying to help. You will be cruel one moment, kind the next—and may even wind up as a fellow victim.

If you cannot find inner peace and maintain it in the face of persecution, you cannot survive. Even a five-year old can learn to dominate you through your emotions. We are all doing each other in with love or hate. We either control, or we are controlled. We are dying through our emotions. Through emotion, we discover death.

Now you know why people are cruel, why they go to such great lengths to upset you. There is a method in their madness. Their cruelty tempts you to judge them; then, the guilt you feel for judging them stresses you to come down from your high horse for acceptance. Before you know it, you are totally preoccupied with the effort to please your manipulators in order to gain their love.

If you are a complete person you have no need to seek completion through others. Whether or not they accept you makes no difference in your well-being. Only wrong people need the support of other wrong people to sustain them.

When others fall all over you with false emotion and praise, don't be tempted for a minute to sample their offering for a bit of selfish pleasure-taking. And when they damn you, be not dismayed. Move neither to the right nor the left—just hold your ground and forbear to judge them. Be unmoved. Stay in your center. When you love the truth, first and foremost, the truth will show you what people are like, and when you see the thing that is expressing itself through them, you won't care what it thinks of you or of anything else. If you can be tempted from your center, either by praise or by blame, your ego has a lesson to learn— namely, the price of "glory."

Anyone who can make you happy has the same power to make you miserable; conversely, whoever can make you miserable has the power to make you happy. He may even do so, if you are careful to oblige him. But what kind of happiness is that? That kind of happiness is to be hated and feared. Suppose the person who makes you miserable delights so much in your suffering that he refuses to ease up and make you happy, no matter how hard you beg. In that case, as long as you look to others for fulfillment you must turn to someone else to make you happy. Then, to that person—your new admirer—you hand over the key to your emotions, and as soon as he discovers his power over you, he will begin to manipulate your feelings, giving or withholding his favors in order to get whatever he wants from you. Manipulation is the game of the damned. They all laugh up their sleeves at your pathetic efforts to "deserve" their "love."

If you *need* the approval of anyone, you make of that person a god—a god who will betray you and cheat you and take liberties. "Falling in love" is indeed falling if you surrender your soul for the illusion of worth that the beloved's acceptance can give you. Your beloved, of course, shares in your fall by reveling in the illusion of worth he derives from his power over you. You can never help the person you are "in love" with—you have made him or her into a god, and the worshiper can never correct the worshiped.

When you are determined to look to others for your completion, your god-making doesn't stop with lovers. You make gods of friends, parents, children—anyone whose "love" you need. Of course, it is easier to observe this god-making weakness in your children when they go overboard for a playmate than it is for you to see your own subservience to your grown-up playmates; but it is precisely because you are both operating under the same outer authority that you cannot help your children. As a victim, a prisoner of the spirit of this world yourself, you cannot but yield to its pressure when it is applied through your children. Few of us fully realize the awesome power of the emotional bonds of love and hate. Love seduces and enslaves, setting us up to hate. Then, feeling guilty for hating, we crawl back for the soothing torments of love. Your love-need makes you weak before your children, whose love you are so afraid of losing that you dare not exert the firm correction they need. They want to be saved from the monster within, but when it expresses itself in your child's violent temper tantrum you simply melt. Its purpose is to upset you into giving in, and you do.

Your children come into the world with a yen, an ego hankering for the supportive affections of others. It takes all the strength you can muster, and God's grace above all, to keep them and yourself from being enslaved to the false god of acceptance. You must be careful, for you can be "had" either way, through love or through hate. The spirit of that love/hate state of being is a life-hungry, energy- and soul-sucking whirlpool. You can't fight it on its own terms. To resist its tricks of accepting and rejecting, you need the true no-need, loving patience of non-reaction. You must find the wholeness within from which a selfless love can flow. You must become part of Him who does not suck in and will not *be* sucked in. Only in this detached-from-the-world, objective state can you hope to survive and save your family. Your children need you *not* to need them, but to shield them with God's saving objective love. If you need the subjective love of your children, you are in terrible trouble. Living in fear that their affection for you can be alienated by strangers, you will fall prey to jealousy, anger, resentment, and guilt. You will be caught in an emotional tug-of-war that will tear your family apart.

True love exists in and through you only to the degree that pride does not. Because emotion is the food of pride, you must not respond to emotion with emotion, to anger with anger, or to false love with false love. It takes a different kind of spirit to overcome the spirit of the world. Don't take pride in seeing yourself as a St. George fighting the dragon, which is what the dragon wants you to feel, for if you win you will *become* the dragon, and if you fail you will become the dragon's slave and lover.

A strange form of love enslaves us to what we hate. Emotion attaches you to your adversary. Feeding your pride, emotion makes you feel like a king while you are nothing but a court jester, trying to elicit praise from your manipulating tyrant with your antics. Are you beginning to see the psychotic thrust of your existence? Controlled by your prideful reactions to the praise, blame, or indifference of others, you are doomed to a lifetime of frustration.

The psychotic use of your talents and skills to engineer acknowledgment from others of your kingship can end only in frustration. Look what happens when you put someone—your husband, wife, or boss—on a pedestal to recognize you, and then you are taken for granted. You take this as a rejection, and you secretly start to resent your elected "authority." Hate, turning to guilt and accompanied by a feeling of failure—which it is, spiritually speaking—drives you to try harder to elicit the show of appreciation you crave. You can be the most talented person in the world, yet not get anywhere on the job or anywhere else because of frustration. Your judgment of a demanding boss who withholds "deserved" recognition may literally drive you to work yourself to death to prove to him he has wronged you. Or you can become so drained by resentment and judgment that you rebel against working at all. Your talents then go unused, as well as unappreciated, and you grow bitter, broken in mind and spirit.

Loving and being loved is as much a hell as hating and being hated. Emotional love, being possessive, always leads to overt or secret hatred of the love object. Look at your infantile need for love and see it for what it is—an ego craving to be God, first as king, then as judge, and finally perhaps, as executioner. See how everything you do is for acceptance and glory, and how it enslaves you to the empty praise of your manipulators.

Children rebel against authority, not only when it is harsh but also when it is timid. A child's ego can smell the weakness behind the emotional needs of pride. It feels the lack of conviction in your confrontation with pressure. Children sense your need for approval, and they know intuitively that you should not be needing theirs. When they pester and whine they are probing for chinks in your armor, and your responses send them the signals they need to spot your particular weakness. When they locate it, they press you to your breaking point, the point at which you will blow up and give in to get rid of the guilt of blowing up. You encourage them to develop an unholy power over you that they know they should not have.

The moment that a child's willful probing "gets" to you is the moment of error, or sin. The resentment you feel in that moment can become so much a part of your ego-survival equipment that you hardly notice its presence; or if you do, you see nothing wrong with it. Your reason rationalizes your sin and locks you into the hell of it with confusing excuses. You say to yourself, "If I'm too strong with them I will drive them to rebel," so you are timid and weak, a pussycat, and they defy you. Now, you try to control them with force and you provoke them to outright rebellion. You are damned if you do and damned if you don't.

The trouble is that your entire life has been fueled by frustration, by the resentments that empower your every move. Even the "good" things you do are a form of response to the pressure of guilt, the result of your having been manipulated by those whose approval you needed. Are you a quiet person, always nice and obliging, a people pleaser, "too good for your own good"? Then it's time to look at yourself. Your niceness is a front to hide your resentment. If you stopped being phony, your rage would burst out. You are quiet to hide your anger from others and from yourself, and you fail to speak up when you should because you fear criticism and anger in others. And you do untold harm. Your failure to speak up gives a silent, nurturing consent to the wickedness in those around you. Of course, you see it as it grows, and you judge it in secret as you savor your superiority to it. Most very quiet people are seething inside with judgment and contempt. They don't speak out because they can't, for fear of losing control and showing themselves to be upset and hateful, thus playing havoc with their self-made veneer of dignified superiority. So they go along with the liberty-takers to "keep them happy." Their "acceptance" of everything wrong can drive husbands, wives, and children up the wall, but the casual observer never sees anything wrong with the maddeningly "nice" ones—only with those they have driven mad.

Then, there is the bubbly personality who takes to everyone, who is always "on" and playing to the crowd. Watch out for this one. Both the quiet ones and the bubbly people-pleasers are love manipulators; but they can be outmanipulated by the worldly-wise.

If you see yourself in either of the above, be warned: Your boss, your mate, or your child will take full advantage of your desire to please and judge. The outmanipulator will simply take advantage of your "goodness" by providing a feast for your resentment and then living it up when you work your tail off for him in order to placate your guilt feelings. Deep down, you always know you are being "had," but you enjoy hating and judging so much that you invite more of the same treatment to give you more reason to hate. You redouble your efforts to please. You work harder and harder, give money and the shirt off your back, even your body, but you are just a slave. You can no more stop bending over backward to please and to serve than your tyrant boss can stop cheating you, or your violent husband can stop beating the hell out of you. Both of you are addicted to your sick emotional needs.

If you see that your kids have turned into monsters, you are either a monster yourself or such a marshmallow that one word from you is a signal to your kids to laugh in your face. Actually, a marshmallow is a monster in disguise. Living in dread of being seen for what he is, he covers up by being super nice. He sees the sense of obligation that drives him as a sign of goodness rather than weakness. His greatest failing—the failing that leads to all others—is his growing craving to be loved and accepted, to be redeemed thereby from the sin of hate. To satisfy this craving he will follow a stubborn course of martyrdom, giving his all to everyone, living the life of an abject slave in his false selflessness, which he proudly construes to be loving service, a way of suffering "for righteousness' sake."

Marshmallow-conformists and monster-rebels justify their respective positions by the wrong each sees in the other. The hypocrite conformists in a family may try to "save" the rebel outcast, but because they need saving themselves, they only make the rebel more rebellious. It is not unusual for what appears to be a loving, concerned family to "do in" the rebel through a kind of hypocrisy that is so subtle and unassailable that it drives him off the deep end. When you read of wanton killings by rapists, muggers, or terrorists, consider that the perpetrators might be "getting even" with the soul-destroying hypocrites whose crimes against them cannot be proved. One reason for their frustration, of course, is that the authorities themselves are so badly infected with the same kind of hypocrisy.

Rarely do we see ourselves as we are. But regardless of what we say or do, our motives show. Our selfishness and pretense cause our children to resent us and their resentment makes them prideful. Their pride then commits them to a life of struggle between conforming and rebelling. Their natural impulse is to wrench free, but they always seal their fate by resenting the evils they see everywhere they look. Eventually, they will either give in to the system and learn to lick the boots of love/hate tyrants or they will go mad, thinking they have finally broken free.

Until you really break free from your mad ego need to be accepted as a god you will set your children up to fill the same mold, and as long as the spirit of original sin remains alive in you, you will pass it on.

When given the opportunity to flower, the good within you is infinitely more powerful than the evil. However, you must see how you are turning your back on the good, forbidding it to enter, through your habit of seeking acceptance from the world and reacting with bitterness from the world's rejection. After all, what is sin but the abandonment of our soul's allegiance to God for the hope of gaining acceptance, somewhere in the world, *as* God. And once a person sins he must forevermore derive his sense of identity, life, and purpose from his new source, his new god. He has appointed an environmental something or someone to God's station, and because that something or someone now forms the source for his belief in himself as the greater god, he will defend that source to the death. Henceforth, he belongs to the system of hell on earth, evolving as one of its "wheeler dealers" or as one of its beasts of burden, conforming for the sake of peace, never questioning the powers that be.

But there is no peace, either for the movers and shakers, the master manipulators, or for the manipulated, the losers. So how do we get out of the rat race? To that question there is only one answer: Resist without resentment, and seek acceptance no longer.

A rebellious person finds it hard to accept the idea of not resenting evil as a means of dealing with it, because he equates "not resenting" with "giving in." To him it's like asking an orthodox Jew to eat pork. Yet anyone should be able to see that standing one's ground and refusing to accept false criteria as "truths" is a far cry from cowardly submissiveness. When you fall to resisting evil through resentment you only perpetuate your need for "love" to justify your fall to evil. Evil meets sin with sin-need and keeps men caged like animals in a dog-eat-dog system where, from the day we are born, we do not draw a sane breath.

Our only escape is to give up resentment. Give up the craving for acceptance and you will never feel hate or frustration. You will never again fall victim to manipulation.

Believe it or not, you *can* rise above your ego-craving for love and hate and discover the salvation of the Lord. All searching souls are blessed with recognition of the Truth. You might even save your family. Not right away, perhaps—it could take years. But while you are waiting patiently, you will be using the fiery confrontations to develop to its fullest the heavenly discipline of patience that alone can stop the worldly will in its tracks.

Don't argue or go to war with anyone. At the same time, separate your loved ones from the wrong spirit in others by means of a no-nonsense, firm, patient demeanor. And ignore the flak!

You need never again experience the emotions of betrayal and frustration. Watch that old surge of resentment in the face of insults. See it for what it is without resenting it or denying its presence. Apologize for it if you recover in time and find it prudent to do so, but as long as the inclination of your soul is in the right direction, simply knowing your own helplessness in each fresh encounter strengthens your prayer to Him Who is not helpless, and the intruder will gradually see that there is no place for it in the house of faith. It's a simple fact that the more you keep company with God, the less you will see of the Devil.

Another thing to watch out for is an all-too-prevalent human tendency to pronounce people "wonderful" especially if they have just reacted enthusiastically to your own personality. Just remember that any reaction to extreme emotions, flattering or cruel, makes it impossible for you to say no to unwarranted demands.

Listen to the tone of voice you use when you tell your children to do something. Are you pressuring them with your willful demands for obedience and respect? Observe your impatience, and see how it upsets your children and makes them feel guilty. See how you take advantage of their guilt, how you then feel guilty, and how they then take advantage of your guilt. See how you are addicting them to your love by upsetting them and then soothing them with favors.

In the past, as you exulted in your pride-fed emotions, your soul was altered, drawn down and changed, rendered responsive to the overshadowing will of darkness. In the future, the eternal now of awareness, as you become objective through a sincere willingness to see yourself as you are, you will be raised up and changed, responsive only to the Light. Good or evil prevails in us and through us in accordance with the inclination of our soul. Through awareness you can give up being cruel one moment, kind the next—manipulated and manipulating.

15

Our Fascination With Falling

The male ego instinctively looks first to the female for the ego support he craves, but the problems he encounters in his pursuit of the female will often drive him to an emotional involvement with alcohol, music, and drugs for that same support. The substitute vices, or comforters, are certainly "safer" in that they do not involve a manipulating female personality.

In the sex-use or abuse of other people, we do become entangled in the confusing maneuvers of contrary personality pressures; but when we escape into the consolations of alcohol, music, and drugs, we encounter an evil that is far more subtle—and not so very much different from the one we are fleeing. Somewhere beyond the experience of the consolation, we run headlong into a lurking personality of an "other" order. We cannot see, touch, taste, or smell it, but it is there nevertheless—a presence, a kind of will-o'-the-wisp greeter, just inside the portals of vice.

Lonely little children invent invisible friends to keep them company. Similarly, the drunk, in his descent from Reality, comes to think of his bottle as his friend, a friend with a personality that "understands" him and communicates with his soul.

But the chemical thing or the musical thing, or even the sex thing, can never, in itself, supply the ego with the supportive understanding it craves. For that it must look to the shadowy intelligence inside the door of vice, an embryonic inner spirit that expresses and develops itself through the wiles of speech, body movement, siren songs and rhythms. Any forbidden experience, such as the use of a drug, opens the door to this evil realm. There, because the soul is spirit, never entirely contained in flesh and blood, it must find the reinforcing, compensatory spirit it craves, or perish. And so it happens that in its fallen state the rebellious soul finds solace through its escape into the forbidden.

While the ego claims its selfish satisfaction through its emotional involvements with people, substances, or music, some intelligent force is using this use of your ego "comforters" as a medium to get inside you. This whole idea may strike you as too shocking and "eerie" even to contemplate, because it may never have occurred to you to realize that your real need is a spiritual one and that the manifestation of wrong is a spiritual matter, the result of a wrong attitude, a lack of true commitment to good. In themselves, drugs can in no way comfort a soul. A drug merely introduces a forbidden experience that rips open the fabric of matter to reveal and release the self-serving genie of the bottomless pit. Your vice represents an escape, of course. But an escape from what? For what? What "values" are you seeking through escape? If you can answer honestly, you will see that you are doing business with hell, giving yourself over to evil for a fleeting moment of relief or glory.

The worldly sin nature can not tolerate a perfect world, not for one moment. It needs a complicated system of evils, intrigues, and distractions in order to reign supreme and secure in the mind realm of its private hell. Vice comforts the soul because it distracts it from seeing the truth of what it has become.

The first order of descent for a man is to marry the kind of woman whose ravishing tease and self-seeking "love" most skillfully captivate his imagination, which will be bound to her later by fascination with her ugliness. Yet, as a kind of natural compensation, the choice of a wrong woman is absolutely right for a vain man. He "chooses" the woman with the familiar indwelling spirit of his mother because the ego of man seeks a soil that will continue to nourish and support it as it was nourished and supported by his mother.

As I have said, corruption is the base of ego existence, and for this reason, evil and death become ever more fascinating as time goes on. So it is that men marry what they richly deserve. Escaping from the corruptive female mother source, the false self that grew from it, fearing correction, refixates to another version of the same thing in a younger supportive female. For a time, he wallows like a pig in the stuff of his own evolving grossness until the awful truth dawns on him: he has made the same mistake his father made. And he thought his father was pretty dumb!

A willful female falls prey to doubts when she is truly and properly loved. She doesn't know how to deal with a decent man because her faith in her wrong self has grown from her associations with weak, condescending men. She really knows how to handle them. She is not so much interested in sex as she is in the secure feeling of power she draws from the fixated victim. Male use and abuse give her a godlike power and a false sense of security. Once addicted to power, she encourages male failing in order to continue playing the starring role in a man's life. To hold onto her self-esteem, she must be his answer, as well as his next problem.

A man digs himself into the same predicament, and for the same reasons, with his use of women as he does with his use of a drug or tobacco. He takes up the habit in the first place as a way of solving a problem, but because he is "solving" his problem by way of escape from realizing he has one, the habit becomes a problem too.

The world offers us an infinite cornucopia of delights with which to serve our ego's need to escape into a prideful sense of fulfillment and worth—delights that blind us to the fact that they are gobbling up our life substance. The bartender gets his security and feeling of worth from selling the booze, while the drunk gets his from drinking it. What chance do we have to survive in a world so full of temptation?

Our one great hope, our saving grace, is the ever-present conscience that we are forever seeking to dope into oblivion and defeat. We see it as our enemy—it surely fails to qualify as a "comforter." It seems always to be "after" us for something we're not ready to give. Yet it is always there, watching, wordlessly nudging us away from the inherent danger of our vices. Have you seen how stubbornly you fight off your conscience and cling to your vices? It is through those vices that the betrayer, the spirit of evil so vital to your proud ego, incarnates itself *in* you *as* you. Even though you may know, through the silent sentry, conscience, that you are being drawn deeper into its hell, the little hell in you is fascinated by the greater hell it is escaping into, and is becoming. You balance precariously between two hells—the hell of facing the truth, and the hell that is drawing you into its velvety folds.

Evil exists in you through your escapes, your comforters, your addictions—the very vices your ego escapes into in order to solve its "problem" of conscience, ever-present, ever-watchful conscience. Do you see how silly it is to pit your transitory escapes against the infinite and incorruptible link to the Creator that your conscience represents? You may flee from it, but you can never really escape it because you can not kill it without totally renouncing your humanity and joining the legions of the damned. Yet, even the evil that is already incarnate within you will resist any effort you might make to understand these words. It could never survive such an understanding, so it immediately sends up a smoke screen to cloud your perception, to brand the written words "pure gibberish," and encourage you to react to them with indignation, resentment, and fear—fear that others might understand them and see you as you are. You may become tired and sleepy, unable to resist the urge to crawl back into your dream world where you can pretend that all is well with you. Oh, don't think for a minute that I am blind and deaf to the hostility my words provoke in some of you, but I persevere because I know that the very fact of your reaction shows that I have hit a nerve, some inner recognition of Truth. Think about it. It's never too late to wake up.

The corrupted self is light-reactive. It reacts to anything good on the outside in the same way it reacts to the presence of conscience on the inside. Your reaction to the words on this page demonstrates the power of words to represent and bring you back to reality. Man was not meant to live in any environment other than His presence, but in our folly we descend into the consoling environment of hell.

Let's see if we can intuit the way it all began. How would you feel if you were the first mortal to fall from grace? Alone with the realization of your folly, could you long endure to contemplate your loss and shame? No. You would soon gravitate to the distractions of food and drink. Then, these natural wants satisfied, you would see your earthly home as a dead-end street, a jail, a tomb. Something deep within your subconscious mind would motivate you to do something to dress up your cell to make it more inviting, more cozy. You would provide it with whatever bits of décor you could find in the environment. Before long, your yearning for still more sensory fulfillment, more reason for being, might cause you to pick up some sticks and discover that you could use them to create a rhythmic noise, pleasing to the ear and the motor senses of your body. As you fixate to the sound and the rhythmic pulsing, the exhilaration of the creative process awakens in you a feeling similar to one you had before you fell, a feeling you thought was lost to you forever. That feeling is hope.

It could all have come about that way, for to this day, music, with its appeal to vanity, retains its power to arouse false hope. Under its spell we lose all awareness of the wretchedness of a life apart from God. Music serves to fill the vacuum; it glorifies the fallen soul and lulls it, drawing it into a dream world where the false hope, ambition, reigns supreme. In your fallen state you fail to recognize ambition as the tempter that got you kicked out of Paradise in the first place.

Those primitive sticks have evolved to a high level of sophistication. Today they are singers and bands, arrayed in great splendor, making sounds that glorify us as kings. Never forget what gives music its appeal, its fascination. It exists to stroke our hungry egos while taking possession of our souls. In an objective state you would recognize music for what it is—a cleverly arranged combination of sounds. There is nothing about music that is conducive to meaningful growth or discovery. You can, if you choose, listen to music in a meaningful way, but where do you look for meaning? Is it in "finding" yourself by losing yourself? Or in resisting the temptation to lose yourself by remaining objective to the tempter, separate from it?

The original appeal to man's ego effected an alteration, not only of his consciousness, but of his physiology as well. Your ability to get "high" on the romantic, exotic, or bizarre sounds of music is a carry-over from that original appeal. Originally, the appeal came in the form of words, words especially crafted to draw the soul outside its protective circle of innocence into Satanic disobedience and servitude to evil. Have you ever really heard what a love song is saying? Have you not noticed how the lyrics, regardless of the culture, are devoted to lust and seduction and the glorification of human weakness, as though it were a virtue? Stand back and observe the force, the intelligence from which it springs.

When you submerge your senses in music you experience a kind of "faith" by way of emotion. Music can create this effect all by itself, but when lyrics are added the words reinforce the spirit of the music. They convey all too clearly the message of that spirit's plans for mankind: madness, violence, revolution, and war. The sincere seeker has little use for music—he can listen to it, abide it without being distracted, or block it out entirely as he carries out his own meaningful activities. To him, Truth speaks in its own wordless way, in its own universal rhythm.

The more music you listen to, the more you doubt the good, and by accepting evil, feel good about your decaying rotten self. Next, you will be drawn to alcohol and other drugs. The sequence of wine, women, and song should be changed to women, song, and wine, for it is the original hang-up with the guileful female that makes us vulnerable to the blandishments of song and wine.

The lie the ego most desires to hear is the one that stimulates the highest impulse of the animal, but the lowest of man, the one that appeals directly to our sensual and romantic feelings. Animal, not human, feelings arise in man each time the soul falls another notch. One of these fallings, or failings, is rage; the other is lust. Man identifies lust with the love of mortal life and the form of woman, the form that arouses that feeling of life. The misguided woman interprets man's lust, his failing for her as well as his abuse of her, as acceptance and even worship. As a result, her pride can not tolerate a truly virtuous man, for such a man does not sacrifice himself to her guile, but stands as a correction to it. He has no "use" for her; and a woman who has been trained to interpret man's use of her as "love" feels that she has been rejected in the absence of that use.

No matter how low a man sinks, he finds a way to glorify each perversity as he falls prey to it. Of course, sex is not necessarily gross, any more than eating is, but the pride in man confuses feelings of need with love, and of rage with righteousness. Instead of observing and modifying his animal weaknesses of need and rage, he uses them for escape. He becomes obsessed with sex and violence. Instead of standing back, observing and learning about himself, he plunges ever deeper into his symptom of failing, the emotion that is increasing his sensitivity to the female and requiring her to "solve" his problem. Through her compliance, of course, the woman also becomes a problem to him: how best to use her.

Here is the formula for the fall: Take one subservient female full of guile; let her appeal to the ego of man by promising him undue sexual favors to "reward" his swinish behavior; add a heaving breast, a womb receptive to his lust, and music to heighten romance and deaden the truth while glorifying the vile deed, and top with a potion of liquor. What man can resist such an offering?

By your folly do you all walk into the jaws of death and hell, thinking you are walking into heaven. No one could warn you before, words failing for want of a true spirit in you to receive them. Even now, you find it difficult to accept the truth, for you are under the spell of a different system of belief, in which the lies of pleasure are far more believable than the words of truth.

Our fascination with deception and death is a back-to-front replica of the fascination we should have with God. In surrender to the Divine, we go through a dissolution of our selfish earthy mind and form. We undergo a gradual transformation from beast to man, from death to life. Knowledge of the way, either to infernal or to eternal life, is deeply encoded in the soul. The life you receive depends on your inclination toward one presence or the other. Death as life and life as life do indeed resemble each other, but true life will elude you until you lay down all selfish fascinations.

Long ago, death appeared when faith in God disappeared. Death as part of life is the mortality man inherits—the ultimate, inevitable truth he must accept as long as the spirit of death speaks to his soul through the grip of vice. During the gold rush days in California, this sign hung over the door of a saloon: *Men are fools, and women merely devils in disguise.* And no one took it seriously. They went on drinking and carousing while the truth stared them in the face.

How about taking a good hard look at the way you defend your self-serving vices. Can't you see that those who truly love you are not involved with you? Nor will they allow you to become involved with them. They are free from you, and they wish you to be free from them. Being inwardly fulfilled, they don't need your emotionality. They leave you free to experience what you must. It is entirely possible that at some point you responded negatively to the extended, but ungrasping, hand of true friendship, just as you have rejected your conscience, and off you went, in search of a false friend and comforter. You may have doubted true love, seeing it as cruel and unsupportive.

You must learn to observe yourself as though you were looking at yourself from a distance. When you do, you will keep some space between you, the observer, and you, the actor, so that you will have time to remember not to get too emotional and close to others. You will not be inclined to get inside them to take anything away. Such objectivity also protects you from being taken over by others, and presto, no more ego-power game. It's over, kaput, finished.

Through the selfless, objective way of focusing your attention you receive love from beyond. When you observe calmly and dispassionately, without fixating, you can neither use nor be used, for you are giving your attention with the kind of love that leads others from hell to heaven.

Of course, from the moment you undertake to live from your common sense rather than from the world's illusions, you will be engaged in a war of natures, yours and theirs, the good coming through your freedom, versus the guile coming through their vices. They will try to make you doubt your perspective in order to involve their nature with yours, but you must frustrate their purpose by remaining calm and detached. The world does not take kindly to the person who can stand alone on principle, so you will be faced with every love/hate trick in the book. Just stand your ground, with merry eyes twinkling.

You must even guard against becoming too close, too involved, with your children, lest they wrap themselves up in your identity and fail to find their own. It is probably impossible for a child not to get involved emotionally with his parents to some degree; but when the parent sets a perfect example, the child will be able, in due time, to transfer his allegiance in a right way to the universal spiritual Parent of us all. Only a loving father can help his child transcend such an involvement and enable him to grow to be a person in his own right. In other words, the child will first reflect the good parent; later, he will become the living reflection of his own conscience.

Just as long as our intent is impure, that long will we remain emotionally involved with folly—people, places, and things— with substitute and supportive parents, the kind who cannot or will not correct us but will always use our need of them.

Our first reaching out to explore the world we find ourselves in is directed by our emotional fascination with the environment and it is based on pride. We take unto ourselves whatever makes us feel good and we reject the rest. But there comes a time when we feel impelled to examine the persona, or self, that our pride has so carefully constructed out of the available material, and at this point, if we are lucky, we will begin to sense a dichotomy between our reconstructed self and the self we might have been born to be. The intensity of the conflict between what we have become and what we might have been—also, its resolution—will depend on whether or not we had a good example, a good role model, to follow. In other words, we will find it easier to transfer our allegiance to the heavenly Father if we had, or still have, a good earthly father to show us the way.

Man is first born of pride through his fixation to the personal and sensual, but he must eventually find humility. The material man gathers his identity through experience, through emotional action and interaction and his involvement with every reassuring thing. But the spiritual man takes his guidance from above (or within) when he renounces his carnal relationship with the world in order to enter into union with God.

God did not create people, beauty, and knowledge in order to provide us with things to get caught up with, but to testify to Himself, the Creator. When you allow yourself to get emotionally involved with the things of creation—the sunrise, the trees, the flowers, sex, even knowledge—you are in effect rejecting God. Giving your entire attention to these things, you die to understanding and are reborn as an animal, and once you are so altered, you can not free yourself from the fascinations that have altered you. You must stay busy and keep moving and continue to cultivate wrong living patterns in order to stay ahead of the truth of your actual failing.

It has been said that "nature abhors a vacuum." If the soul is not filled in one way, it will be filled in another. Your soul will become fixated in the direction toward which it inclines. Do you love God? Or would you rather "play" God? To be or not to be—that is indeed the question. To be, you must resolve in your heart not to *be* God, but to obey Him.

16

How Compensations
Lead to Death,

the Ultimate "Comforter"

The urge for liberation, or release, is so prevalent in our devolving society that psychologists had to give it a name. They call it the "death wish" or "death instinct." Unfortunately, they have never come up with a satisfactory explanation for it. Why should people will their own death?

The death wish—the will to be liberated from the prison of the body—begins with a desire to be liberated from the inhibition of conscience. Near the end of life's journey, or even not too far from the beginning if it has been a bad trip, the guilt of the way we have been existing becomes so unbearable that many of us develop a need to be liberated from the body itself. That leaning toward death is a phenomenon so widespread that it is familiar to most of us. How often have you heard someone ask "Who wants to live forever?" as though eternal life would be an unbearable burden. And of course it would be to the soul that insists on playing God. Sooner or later, he is bound to make mistakes, and as the evidence of his having done so piles up around him he longs to get away from it all. To him, losing face is worse than facing death.

If, at any point, we could be arrested in our headlong plunge toward death and made aware of the fact that we have been running from the best friend we ever had, the conscience that bonds us to our Creator, we might actually experience the liberation of the soul that is known to the religious community as salvation. Yes, salvation, that favorite word of the ministers and sidewalk preachers. Even though you might be a regular churchgoer, have you ever taken that word seriously? Have you considered how it might affect your real life, your daily comings and goings? Have you even seen the connection between conscience and salvation?

If you have thought about salvation at all, haven't you relegated the realization of it to some remote future time, after you have had ample opportunity to enjoy the delights of the world and stuff yourself on its goodies? You may even have associated it with death—mother Death, tucking the comforter around your well-filled tummy as you nod off from a world that you will never have to face again. Oh, salvation from the world might have seemed a good idea to you, but you certainly didn't want it before its "time"—that is, before you had lived it up (experienced the world) so thoroughly that you had lost all interest in looking back on the shambles.

We all have a choice to make—to grow in pride and become a mortal beast, or to grow in some yet unknown way as a real person. The way we choose will take us through stages of development and changes of personality so opposite and foreign, one to the other, that in time we will totally forget the other way and how we happened to choose the path we are now on.

While I might not be able to prove it scientifically, I am convinced that the choice was made for us by our prideful reaction to the shock of trauma, and a steady diet of trauma has sustained our growth in the "chosen" direction. Unfortunately, because we have all inherited the "choice" of pride from Adam, we all elect to take the downward, sinful way of pride with its willful rationalizations and compensations until the sheer pain of living with the results either drives us back to conscience and the hope of salvation, or makes us yearn for death, the last ray of hope for the damned.

The selfish gambler keeps returning to the casino, not only to make up for his past losses, but to prove to himself that he can beat the odds and strike it rich. Of course, the hope for gain leads inevitably to the next loss and whets his appetite for gain. We resemble the gambler in our addiction to the proud way of the world in that it was our inherent pride and greed that laid us open to the original trauma, the sin experience that left us with a sense of loss and changed the bright nature we might otherwise have clung to. Most of us have been set up to fail by our proud, ambitious parents and teachers. Any proud, resentful reaction to a real or imagined challenge to our ego might have started us out on the wrong foot, and most of us can endure an incredible amount of suffering before we can be persuaded to renounce the way of pride.

Our failings, or offenses against conscience, I call "sin," the agent of destruction that gradually deforms the soul and subjects the body to disfigurement. As we persist in the forbidden way of pride, we grow guilty and we take on an altered identity. Our pride forces us to relieve our guilt by accepting as "good" every evil we fall prey to. In other words, we learn to compensate; i.e., to make up for our loss of virtue with some parallel equivalent as measured by our altered system of values. As the soul falls through trauma, it seeks to make up its loss, or at least to mask it by calling the good "evil," and the evil "good." Our efforts lead only to futility, of course, for we can not possibly make up for the brightness we have lost from above in the gross animal that is evolving below. All losers are great compensators. A failing man, for instance, compensates with machismo, and a woman who has lost her bright nature adopts an exaggerated air of femininity.

We may compensate for our deep-seated unhappiness with a sparkling sense of humor; for our inner poverty with the acquisition of riches; for our lack of wisdom with much learning; for our inferiority feelings with achievement; for our secret failings with phony goodness. We are forever seeking substitutes for the real thing; but no facsimile, no pretense, no goal or talent can ever make up for the missing element of goodness that constitutes eternal life. Any attempt to substitute some worldly experience for a spiritual lack is just another failing. As though we had the power to give ourselves anything! As though we could make up from below what we have lost from above! Can you possibly imagine the kind of person you might have been had you not stroked yourself with your compensations? Your prideful struggle to make up—out of the intellect, the earthy, the sensual and gross—an equivalent for the gift of life you spurned is sheer folly. Do you see it now? And, seeing it, would you rather die *from* it or *to* it?

As things stand now, you are probably a slave to the compensation process. Drinking, for instance—a compensation— merely intensifies the fears and insecurities that the drunkard was trying to escape, with the result that the more he drinks, the more he has to drink. Because your stubborn pride is constantly compensating for its failures, you become enslaved to your compensations, your comforters, your addictions.

I have said that the sin that makes a home in you is, in part, an emotional trauma, the result of a wounding emotional experience that has changed your soul, the wellspring of your being. And because the change is for the worse, you feel it as a deepening sense of loss, inferiority, and guilt. Let me say it again. Should you refuse to look at the fact that you have failed by taking the wrong path in life, and should you persist in seeing the creature of compensation you have become as the one and only real "you," then you will continue to be drawn to vice and sin. Your stubborn pride will enable you to continue enjoying your particular form of "life" support, and I won't be able to help you.

You can complete your identity in one of two ways. You can go on completing the compensating animal self that came into existence through trauma or failing; or you can see what your compensations have done to you, repent of the power you gave them, and seek to renew your rapport with the conscience within. A negative state of mind caused you to seek compensation for your loss of faith. It compelled you to go on failing in order to "perfect" the "virtue" of pride in the fallen animal flesh. If you had not failed, or fallen away from the dictates of conscience, you would not have felt driven to compensate for the failure through any means at your disposal. For instance, the alcoholic soon discovers that if he can needle his wife into upsetting him, his anger will somehow justify his drinking and enhance his enjoyment of it. He can even blame her for driving him to it. In time, he becomes dependent on resentment in order to put an edge on his drinking pleasure, the comforter he "allows" himself to indulge in as compensation for his lost happiness and innocence.

To choose the other way, the right way, you must first see, clearly and objectively, the connection between your need to compensate yourself for the loss and the loss itself, whether you are consoling yourself with the bottle or with some more acceptable form of compensation, like becoming the world's greatest intellect or lover. What it was that got you started on your downward course matters very little. It might have been your own inherent greed or pride or the degrading influence of others. A willful parent or guardian might have laid an ego trip on you by causing you to doubt yourself. Or it might have been the way you responded to a simple dare or some other challenge to your pride.

You may be confused as to your intent, mistaking the ambitions your mother implanted in you as your own, always trying to become something other than the person you were created to be. Or you might have lent money to someone you trusted, and when he failed to pay you back you became so embittered and preoccupied with thoughts of revenge that you jumped the track and were never able to get your life back "on course." No matter. Until the time of enlightenment, *all* experiences involve descending and compensating, even compensating for our compensations.

God granted us the freedom from conscience that enables us to defy it in order to grant us the opportunity to learn the lessons of life from our own experience. Like Pinocchio, we must be free to learn the lessons that can be best learned by leaving the marked path. Rebelling, defying conscience, living as we "choose," failing as we rise, and compensating as we fall, we experience the pain of separation from the real self and, depending on the degree of our awareness, the futility of our efforts at compensation. The experience of liberating ourselves *from* conscience can teach us to value the true liberation *of* conscience. So it is up to each one of us to learn the great truth for himself. No one can reveal it to us because we will not believe it until we are ready to believe it. And we will not be ready to pull ourselves away from our comforters until we have suffered the consequence of having fallen to them.

For a time—too long a time for most of us—locked into the ego life of pride with its craving for worldly comforts, we forget the way of true life. We lose ourselves in a very deadly game. You wanted adventure and excitement? You get it—along with the misery that is part and parcel of that way of life. Unless, at some blessed moment of awareness you see where your "freedom" is leading and seek to break your fall, you will continue to spiral downward until, at the end, after you have experienced every forbidden thing, all you will have left to long for and comfort yourself with is death itself. The liberation that begins with freedom from conscience leads you by degrees to the death wish. Your urge to free yourself from your decaying body can make you want to jump out of your skin, literally, away from the horror of what you have become.

At many points on its descending course, your soul is offered a crucial choice, an opportunity to repent and return to conscience. You have tried "freedom" and have experienced to some degree (though not yet to the point of no return) the "rewards" of a "free" life. You have surely suffered, and whereas the suffering might have softened your heart, it has hardened it. Then, the hardening of your heart caused you to go on compensating and your efforts to recoup your losses have increased your guilt and driven you to still more compensations.

When you see, in one of those magical moments of insight, the evil identity that first tempted and now manifests itself in you, you must realize that this altered creature is not the real you. Otherwise, your pride will compel you to identify with, and love, this false self, and you will see your own conscience, standing ready to receive you back, as your mortal enemy. It is pride, of course, that evil demon so beloved of our culture, whose interests are at stake here, for it was pride that justified and gratified you at each stage of descent. Suddenly to see and to realize that the "best" of your accomplishments, your laboriously achieved compensations, are alien to your real identity, after you have wasted your life cultivating them (accumulating money, developing talents) is a wake-up experience that will call on you for the greatest degree of detachment and objectivity you can possibly muster, and you will need grace to do it. Salvation can be yours if you cultivate that state of detachment through right meditation.

Remember that you can "perfect" your identity in either of two ways. You can go on to death, stubbornly completing the brutish self that came into existence through trauma; or you can realize the truth, shrink from worldliness, give up your prideful attachments through detachment, and so become a true survivor.

The first course requires you to go on failing so that the spirit of compensation can develop to its fullest power and thus complete the fallen identity in you. As long as you refuse to look at this ongoing process that is transforming you into a being that is not the real you, but is the creation of compensation, willfully fashioned of the stuff of pride to make up for spiritual loss, you will continue to be fascinated by people who are only too glad to help you fail. Through their "love" and "help" you will continue to devolve on the journey to your ultimate "comforter," death. (Ah, "freedom" at last—goodbye, cruel world !)

My hope in writing this, of course, is to construct a mirror of words, so graphic and true to reality, that if you can see yourself in it you will be so horrified at what has happened to you on the road you have chosen that you will seek a new direction quite naturally, without having to "will" it pridefully. As a matter of fact, the very first step is just plain giving up, "letting go," as the mystics say, "and letting God."

The life of pride proceeds from an involvement with deception, even as the life of humility proceeds from the love of truth. While you are immersed in the prideful way of life, you respond to, and develop from, falsehood and sham as though it were gospel. So whatever subtle deception caused you to fail in the first place will eventually come to live within your compensated personality. There, it will go to work to cloud your perception and persuade you to see failing as a virtue, a means of becoming a very important person. The metaphysical essence of deceit that caused you to fall will continue to make trauma and compensation attractive to you. Under its spell, you will become adept at explaining away truth with what appear to you to be "well-reasoned" excuses. Your life will be one long process of sinning and excusing. Your vices will grow, not only from the original trauma, but also from whatever it is that you grow to see as the "real" problem behind any shortcoming.

For instance, you might decide that the only reason you were not selected to be the prima ballerina of the company stems from the director's dislike of you, whereas you might never have become a ballerina in the first place if your brothers and sisters hadn't delighted in calling you "clumsy" and thus launched you on a crusade to "show" them how wrong they were. You may have forgotten that initial resentment entirely, but you soon became so accustomed to depending on resentment for motivation that you have used it to run your life. If they had called you stupid, you might have become a perennial student and amassed a string of meaningless degrees—meaningless because you betrayed your common sense to get them. Who knows what you might have become if you had learned early on to listen to the promptings of your inner self, if you had not allowed your inborn faith in divine guidance to be so easily upset by the careless words of others?

Whatever it was that started you down a road that was wrong for you, you may be absolutely sure that resentment had a hand in it. You were hurt, yes, but the real damage was caused not so much by the hurt as by your resentment of it. First, resentment; then, compensation.

You couldn't bear the fact that someone saw your weakness, your Achilles' heel, so you had to make a liar out of him; and with every toss and turn in your bed of resentment, you advanced the gears of compensatory change another notch. If you had not been intimidated by someone smarter, richer, meaner and stronger than yourself, more talented, better looking—whatever—and had you not resented the fact that you were made to feel so low and inferior, you would never have compensated. You would never have felt the need to do so because you would be a person who lives by intuitive faith in his inner prompting and such a person is not highly reactive to the world outside. Indeed, who can serve two masters?

It takes the strong emotion of resentment to generate the energy required for the fabrication of a compensatory covering of thoughts, words, and deeds. Resentment is the devolutionary stuff upon which you have built your whole rotten, hypocritical life. It won't be easy for your pride to give up wallowing in the muck of its hard-won compensations—your degrees, your phony goodness, your money, your accomplishments. To do so would be to die—to the world.

Let's look at another ploy pride uses to pull us off our moorings and start us on the downward journey. Suppose, for instance, you choose as a role model someone you admire for his ability but secretly hate for his air of superiority. Your undercover resentment seeds in you a need to compensate to the degree that you feel inferior to the admired/hated object. As time goes on, the energy of your resentment will continue to feed in you some "strength" that is equivalent to, or greater than, the role model's as you seek to equal or surpass him in "worth."

In order to become like, as good as, or better than someone else, you must have this love/hate relationship with him. You may keep your resentment secret and appear to love the love/hate object, but your show of love is merely a ploy designed to support his false sense of worth and give you an excuse to hate him more. You need the powerful emotion of hate to empower you in the strenuous "work" of compensation. As resentment sets in, you feel a strange surge of energy, a gratuitous impulse of hope, of "life." The game of intrigue breathes into you the false life you were seeking and your continuing resentment helps you to stay ahead of your conscience, blind and deaf to what you are becoming.

Perhaps you understand now what I mean when I say that you become like what you hate. How could it be otherwise? You are deriving your entire energy for growth from your hateful reaction to the hated/loved object. The only kind of love you will ever be able to extend to anyone will be pejorative, the kind that is guaranteed to make him worse, thanks to your subconscious need to go on hating and surpassing him.

Do you understand? Have you seen anything of yourself in the mirror I have been holding up for you? Do you see how your own pathetic development might have proceeded from your resentment (hatred) of the superior qualities you envied in someone else?

Through envy and resentment you try to draw another person's "worth" into yourself, and by doing so you destroy your own birthright. If your emotion had not robbed you of the ability to see clearly, you would see that the person you have been trying so hard to emulate is nothing but a wretchedly compensated person himself, a failure, all dressed up with nowhere to go, with no other purpose but to tempt you, too, to be one of hell's own. Conscious, prideful choices, made with prideful effort, to be "more" than you are simply make you less of what you were meant to be.

You are descending, not climbing, as you "succeed" at becoming like what you hate, assuming another's identity to fill the place made empty by your abandonment of self through hate and pride. Now you see why the intellectual is often so neurotic, lopsided, devoid of common sense and confused—and why he is so confusing to those who have not yet lost their common sense to an over-developed intellect. Here we see a person who is capable of inventing highly sophisticated computers but is a complete dunce about household finances and incapable of raising a family. The poor fool has displaced his real self, with its innate wisdom, to make room for a borrowed identity.

Remember, as long as you see fit to comfort yourself with the emotion of resentment, it will pressure you over and over again to become like the hated person. Consider the case of a young girl who feels inadequate as a woman. She has probably forgotten the original hurt, the one that first triggered her resentment. It might have been at the hands of her ambitious, masculine, overbearing mother; if so the last thing the girl wants is to be like her mother; but, try as she might, as long as she continues to grow on the energy engendered by hating her mother, she can grow no other way but in her mother's image. Now, horrified at seeing that she is growing masculine inside, just like her mother, she tries to compensate by looking and acting extra feminine on the outside. Alas, she gets it all wrong. With a role model like her mother, she has no concept of true femininity. She thinks (from watching television, perhaps) that femininity means being aggressively exciting to men, a temptress, so that is what she becomes in her attempt to become more womanly. Of course, her aggressive seductiveness attracts only the weakest, least masculine of men. She is caught in a vicious cycle, set in motion by her resentment of her mother. Had she not resented her mother's domineering ways, she need not have grown in her image and become masculine herself. Now she resents her weak lovers for their failure to restore to her the feminine identity she seeks.

She is frustrated; her plan has backfired. First, she feels anger, then resentment, inadequacy, and guilt. Guilt leads her back to trying to make up, or compensate, in some way—and what "better" way is there but to try harder to be more of a woman (more aggressive) with a man? Every time she tries to implement her decision, of course, she encounters another exchange disaster. As she continues to compensate by seducing weak men, she becomes more masculine herself, more compelled to compensate for the man growing inside her by becoming more seductive outside.

Surely you already know that some of the most innocent appearing people are the most conniving and wicked inside. Even so, some of the most feminine-appearing women are the most masculine inside. As people grow old and tired of playing games, they let it all "hang out," and the exchanged identities emerge for all to see: old men who look like old women, and old women who look like old men.

No doubt about it—the need to compensate springs from failure, some failure to live up to what your pride expects of a "god" like you. The more ambitious you are, the more strenuously you try to compensate for the failing of your ambitions, and the more you involve yourself with sin's inner process of deterioration and death. For a time, you may be able to conceal from others, and even from yourself, what you are becoming inside; but the sin-converted identity growing up inside you will press ever more forcibly to convert the visible, as well as the hidden, into its own likeness. The body you now inhabit in no way resembles the incorruptible body you were meant to have. All your changes have taken you away, step by step, from your original God-given brightness; and sooner or later the truth of what you have become must break through the façade—in the form of madness, perhaps, or cancer, or in some other dread form.

The conflict you feel is evidence, both of failure and of your unwillingness to face the fact of failure. All compensations are productive of conflict because they are wrong answers to conflict. Compensating is merely a veneer, a pretense, a fig leaf for the sin that has made a home in you. The false fulfillments you pursue so avidly for the sake of your compensations can lead only to a greater sense of loss, of shame, of inferiority, of guilt. Finally, just as you can compensate through the resentment of others, you can turn that resentment against yourself, and so metamorphose again through being angry at yourself. At this stage, the evil buried deep inside appears in your animal flesh.

Do you see that, no matter how hard you try to compensate, you are involved with a process of exchange? And that the sin growing up inside you as a result of the first exchange uses emotion to convert the compensated flesh into its own likeness, so that you begin to look like the devil? To compensate, you must be ambitious and prideful, and you must fail, you must sin, you must be hateful, resentful, and pridefully competitive—until you become the image of evil.

While your soul is compensating, evil is eating away at your fleshly being from within. Any compensation for failing is as much a failing of the ego, as much a sin, as the failing that led to the compensation in the first place. Compensation is the beast made manifest in the flesh.

Think about it. Take a good, long, objective look at yourself and see that you can not make up for anything that you are not. You cannot make yourself good or clever or brave.

Now that you know where failing leads, let your conscience catch up with you and set you free before the ultimate compensation, the ultimate "comforter" of the unrepentant, Death, overtakes you.

Epilogue

Just say the magic word "sex" and you command the attention of everyone in range of your voice. No matter how much you know about it—love it, hate it, or fear it—nothing is more charged with mystery, or more appealing to our curiosity, than sex. Yet one of its little mysteries is hardly ever mentioned in spite of the fact that most of us have caught fleeting glimpses of it at one time or another. The connection is so subtle that you might have thought you were mistaken in your awareness of it. In any event, you probably haven't tried to pin it down.

Until I was fourteen years old, I knew nothing at all about sex. You might say that I was innocent. But during my fourteenth year, I was living in a boarding school, World War II was in full sway, and food was rationed along with just about everything else, especially in England. One night, I got so hungry that I slipped downstairs into the forbidden zone and stole some cookies out of the pantry. Presto: sexual awakening.

I hadn't thought much about that phenomenon until recently when it struck me like a bolt of lightning that there is a distinct connection between sin and human sexuality. The trauma of sin produces an altered state of consciousness, sexuality enters, and with it a strange new consciousness of self—in need of a fig leaf.

Let's examine the mechanism behind sexual awakening. You have heard it said that power corrupts, and that absolute power corrupts absolutely. Let me add that power is also the ultimate aphrodisiac. In the corruption process, purity is violated; that is, the pure gives place to the impure, and the morality consciousness falls from a more nearly perfect to a definitely more *imperfect* state. To corrupt is to violate, to introduce trauma, or sin. And if corruption, or trauma, is to take place it must have a trauma source, the psychological term for what we used to refer to as a temptation or a tempter.

Could it be that, at least where mankind is concerned, sexuality is unnaturally natural? Could it be that falling to, believing in, or experiencing the guidance of any source other than original conscience results in the death of the original man or woman, and the resulting loss of innocence rouses the animal being and opens the senses to the world? It could be, couldn't it? As in "Adam's eyes were opened...and he saw that he was naked."

Something certainly happened to bring down Adam's consciousness, and it also affected his biological self. Look back over your own life to see whether such a thing might be repeating itself subtly within you. What exactly *is* this sin? Well, sin is anything that gives you a "high," anything that enables you to feel good, like God, or anything that makes you feel powerful and right when you are wrong, like judgment.

Cruel people tease you to hate, and the violation awakens a sexual feeling in you that calls out for their approval. The moment you fall to the temptation to hate, you become separated from your inner wholeness of being and you are changed psychologically to seek sensual completeness with your tormentor. The violator, in turn, seeing your eagerness to submit to his intimidation, experiences the sexual elixir of power.

If any of you men have ever had a fight with your wife and wound up dominating the situation, you must have noticed a tendency toward erection. The sin of the teaser tyrant is to indulge the forbidden experience of power by seeking out and terrorizing the weak and the gullible.

Do you see now how power corrupts, and why it is the ultimate aphrodisiac? Notice how the weak fall and give power to the "strong," and how this power awakens the ego-sexual beast, which then upsets and violates its victim.

In a manner of speaking, the cowardly victim contributes to his own violation by awakening in the bully an insatiable appetite for power. The need for power is so addictive that the more the bully gets the more he needs, and he feeds on the terror he arouses in his victim for sexual feeling. So you see it is as much a sin to allow yourself to be violated as it is to enjoy violating.

The victim always experiences a psycho-sexual need for the sexual "love" of the violator. The violator's "love" is the only love compatible with the psycho-sexually awakened need in the victim, so all who are violated unconsciously seek association with those who will violate them. They see violation as love and completeness for their being.

Needless to say, you hate your violator just as you did your first trauma source, but you are no longer the same person. Your "spirit" is different. It cries out to be violated, for to be violated is to be more "complete." The more completely violated a person is, the more completely corrupt he is, but that is the only way he knows how to exist.

Hate is the emotion you felt when you were first violated, but hate is the sin that separates you from God's indwelling love and opens you to sensual, violating love. Your yearning is your psychic need crying out for the violator to violate you. The violator, in turn, experiencing *power*, falls into sexual lust, and his love violates you. So the hate self within you joins once more with the violator and feels completed. But because the completed self is a degraded self in the light of Reality, your guilt draws you to deny the truth by immersing yourself in the false sexual love of the degrader over and over again. Actually, it is hard to tell who is the "demoralizer" and who is the "demoralizee."

Remember that the man who feels the aphrodisiac of power is becoming addicted to what appears to be a submissive person, but one who is actually beginning to turn the tables on him. If you examine the *modus operandi* of the average whore, you can see how the power play goes into reverse and ends by favoring the whore, the one who "appeared" to be the victim initially. And when the man becomes aware of his emasculation, his powerlessness *vis-à-vis* his "victim," he may fly into a violent rage. The object, of course, is to terrorize the woman back into submission and thus give him back his aphrodisiac of power. But when the woman is not a whore, not in whorish control of the situation, but submitting perhaps from a sense of wifely duty, it is she who has the power, inasmuch as the man becomes aware of how he is dehumanizing himself through his own acts of degradation. She fails to give him the feedback he requires for his bestiality, so he ends by feeling mysteriously out-degraded and outranked, and may try even harder to regain the upper hand by beating her into a pulp. But he can't win for losing. The very fear of his battered victim drives him to greater bestiality, and as he becomes more of a beast, he becomes less of a man.

As long as we are fallen beings we will continue to seek fulfillment of our sexual being with our missing other half. And who might that be? Who else, in the case of a man, but the woman most like the mother who first degraded him through her cruelty, confusing signals, or false love? As for a woman, she will always gravitate to a man like the father who either failed her or violated her. Sexual feeling always calls out to the violator, first the parental object of hate, and then the spousal object of hate. By experiencing our "love" for each other sexually, we turn each other into beasts.

Please understand me. You must not construe anything I have said here to mean that sex is wrong or unnatural. The basic dynamics of which I have spoken are universally true, but most of us become aware of the dangers lurking on the dark side of our psyche before we give ourselves over so completely to the quest for sexual gratification that we become monsters. If you have read me right, and if you are completely honest with yourself, you can relate to what I have said by reflecting on the kind of woman you find attractive. What qualities does she have that arouse you sexually, probably to the point of addiction?

Answer: You will always be excited by, and attracted to, a deeply disturbed female, because almost without exception, such a person has been rejected and degraded, perhaps even sexually abused, by her father. Even though she might not have been sexually violated by her father, she has come to hate him so much for some other offense, real or imagined, that she has cut herself off from the possibility of a natural inner unfolding and has instead "come alive" to an external source of the corruption that is embodied in the need for "love" or fulfillment through the senses. (Freud was right about this incestuous need for a father's love.) The father the little girl hated is the father she wants to please sexually, and as she sees her father in all men, she transfers this sexual need to them. For her, all men are violators, and all men become objects of her secret loathing. You men experience this loathing the morning after the night before—do you recognize it? You love her, and she hates you, and you scratch your wooden head in wonder.

Like the drug pusher, who nurtures the addict for evil power, a violated woman submits for power while nurturing a man's selfish, even criminal, behavior. The false love that comes through the false submission of a female nurtures what is wrong in the man and develops in him such a craving for that false love that he is driven to violate her for its satisfaction. What has "gone wrong" in the woman nurtures and "loves" what is also wrong in the man;

and that which has "gone wrong" in the woman is her original hate reaction to violation that she now equates with "love." Hence, her addiction to sensual love is an addiction to hate. The violated woman is addicted to hate, addicted to rekindling, in each new experience, that original contempt for all men. For that reason, she allows a succession of unprincipled cads to abuse her. In the case of the first one or two, she may have wistfully hoped to find real love, but when she finds none, her disillusionment whets her hunger for the power and false sense of superiority that she can find in submission, degrading the degrader in order to feed her contempt for all men as they are represented in him. What she needs, although she may not know it, is a decent man to stop her downward slide, to be kind, to extend to her the true love that she expected, but never received, from her father.

But where do you find a man strong enough to resist the forbidden fruit that dangles so seductively from so many branches?

Well, gentlemen, that is your problem. That ability to resist temptation and to overcome your own sexual lust is the one attribute, the one quality, you must find. As long as you cling to your sensual weaknesses, every violated woman you are attracted to will spot them and she will view your every overture as tantamount to abuse. All such women (and don't forget that they are the ones who will attract you) are addicted to hating men, and the trauma of hate awakens their need to encourage man's sexual appetite to the point of abuse. There you have the psychology of "loving to hate." Have you never known a person you loved to hate?

What I have been detailing here is the classic love/hate relationship. The bottom line, as I noted earlier, is that it is trauma, or sin, that awakens sexuality and the capacity to experience sensual life to the fullest.

It might help you to see the sin/sex connection more clearly if we examine the way it can work in a situation where only one sex is involved. For instance, a mother can be so utterly cruel to her own daughter that the girl's reaction to the trauma awakens in her a sexual feeling for her own mother, the source of the trauma—and hence, the trigger for the reaction. Now, because her sexuality awakened through a female violator, she will be female-oriented, ripe for the plucking, either by the mother herself or by the first mother substitute, or woman with lesbian leanings who senses the girl's need and gratifies it sexually. The way things develop from this point on will determine whether or not the girl will ever seek to adapt to a normal lifestyle. After all, the very process of nurturing the newly-awakened sexual need constitutes an extension and deepening of the original trauma. It is one thing to traumatize a child, or anyone else, with cruelty, but to nurture and encourage the newly-awakened need is to carry things to an even more evil extreme. The first awakening is a shock from which recovery might be possible, but the nurturing of the new need for a person's own sexual gratification is highly addictive. Each new level of excitement in the fall from innocence is as traumatic as the original sin that set it in motion.

If you tease someone enough to upset him into developing hate-based sexual feelings for you, and then proceed to nurture those feelings, you are encouraging the sin-self you have implanted in him to become dependent on you for lying sexual love, the "love" that kills. And you will notice that little sexual sinners are always addicted to, and dominated by, the big sexual sinners.

Perhaps the foregoing will help you to understand the dynamics involved in addictions to pornography, failed marriages, and the tendency to seek love in all the wrong places for all the wrong reasons.

Do you see now how the sin-sex connection explains sado-masochism? As we degenerate we require ever more sophisticated cruelty and tease to awaken sexual feelings. Once a person has been violated he can no longer experience natural love with natural sexual responsibility. He has to be awakened by a violation of some kind. No violation=no "love."

The same principle applies to the women who put up with abusive husbands. From them they get the only kind of love they have ever known, and the only "love" they know how to give back springs from their hatred for cruel men.

Alcoholism, even, can be seen as a form of pseudo-masochism. You see, the alcoholic, whose only happiness is the "love" he gets from his bottle, has to be upset or traumatized in some way in order to open his senses and deepen his capacity to enjoy the drink to the fullest extent possible. The drink brings him the "love" that fulfills his alcoholic being and provides him with his only happiness, the relief of pain. So it turns out that all addictions, each new one evolving from the one before it, start with a person's being violated, then outraged, then having to wallow in the addictive hang-up for relief. The relief itself, as we have seen, is another form of violation that reawakens the need to be violated. Hence, we indulge in sex to forget the pain and guilt-of indulging in sex, and we drink to forget the pain and guilt of drinking, and we eat...ad infinitum. And as each addiction fails to gratify, and eventually causes more pain than it cures, we look to lower experiences for excitement. And there is always another violator out there waiting to answer our need the minute we're ready for his ministrations.

Vast numbers of people get caught up in this devolutionary process and wind up no better than beasts, violating and being violated, lusting and being lusted after, and torturing one another for the sexual pleasure of degrading and being degraded all the way to the grave. All too often it is their violator who has put them there, for only the dead can never out-degrade or out-class their "lover," and murder, the final act of utter sexual domination, is a powerful aphrodisiac.

The Foundation of Human Understanding

Just as the legendary Sherlock Holmes brandished a magnifying glass in order to more closely examine evidence in the solving of a mystery, each of us needs to learn how to examine our own thoughts through the magnifying glass of the objective mind. In many ways similar to a Sherlock Holmes mystery novel, each of our lives is wrought with various episodes of love, hate, betrayal, revenge, contempt, power, weakness, loyalty, compassion, forgiveness, and the whole spectrum of human emotional experience. And without your ever realizing it, these various emotional experiences (mostly traumas) have actually served as a blueprint for problems you now have and the type of person you have become. However, through the process of observation/concentration, or objective inner exploration, you can transcend the negative emotional experiences of the past and regain the reward of living "happily ever after." Ultimately, the most difficult decision you must make is whether or not you really want to deal with the pain of the past, and finally overcome the hidden or perhaps forgotten traumas that lead to your present problems, confusion, and failures.

If you have tried other self-help techniques without lasting or meaningful results, Roy Masters' simple and effective method will finally allow you to uncover and dispel the subtle, causative factors that have mysteriously held you back from living your own life. Surely we all know or at least sense deep within, that damaged or missing bits and pieces of ourself of our mind, heart, and soul, need to be healed if we are to go on to live fulfilling, normal lives. But for many, the nightmare never ends because the missing pieces of the puzzle are never sought and the answers we so vitally need to know are never found. No wonder we futilely seek to procure happiness and fulfillment from possessions, experiences, and others. Failing to grasp our own identity and discover the true purpose for our own lives leaves us unable to find our own unique direction. If you have read this far, by now you will have begun to see that what is preventing you from achieving your true potential, finding security, self- confidence and success, is the simple understanding about why you have become the person you are today. Without this knowledge, you will find it literally impossible to be at peace with yourself. Because without this knowledge the unresolved mystery of your despair will linger in your mind, ever in need of the keys of truth to unlock the doors of your mind so the real you can be set free.

Over the past 30 years, Roy Masters, lecturer, writer, radio talk show host, and founder of The Foundation of Human Understanding, has scientifically examined the problems common to all people, and discovered the missing keys that can enable those who are ready to be free of the mind's negative emotional blocks. Once understood, the process known as observation/concentration, which is the cornerstone of Masters' teachings, is extremely simple to use and totally effective in bringing you to the understanding and forgiveness, that enables you to shed the traumatic conditioning of your past.

As you slowly search through the clues of your past, you will systematically uncover the riddle of your true identity. You will begin to find and assemble the missing pieces of the puzzle, and as you do, you will begin to recognize the negative facets of your personality you have adopted from others. As this takes place over time, your mind, body, and soul will heal from deep within. Now it is just a matter of choosing between the life you now lead and the life of happiness and well- being that is waiting just ahead. It doesn't matter what your age is. It doesn't matter what you do, what you are, or what you have been. All that matters is that you begin the journey so that you can become yourself, and come to understand your own personal destiny and real purpose for being.

FHU, P.O.Box 1009, Grants Pass, OR 97526. Tel.: 1-800-877-3227

Other books by Roy Masters

In each of his books, Roy Masters focuses on the relationship that exists between your emotional reactions and the quality of your life. In each book you find insights that enable you to meet life's stresses with greater objectivity than you ever thought possible.
All book are quality paperback.

The introductory package: How Your Mind Can Keep You Well
Simple instructions in the basic technique of observation-concentration taught by Roy Masters. The package consists of three compact cassettes and the 201-page book of the same name. Price: $49, includes 1st class mailing.

How Your Mind Can Keep You Well
This introductory book teaches you the basic Observation/Concentration exercise
that leads to effortless self-discipline. It is composed of simple instructions in a relaxing technique that enables you to eliminate fear and anxiety from your life. 201 pages, $9.95.

How to Conquer Negative Emotions.
Second in the series, this book concentrates on showing you how to uncover and neutralize the effects of past emotional trauma on your present life, thus freeing you
to deal with today's problem today. 325 pages, $9.95.

How to Conquer Suffering Without Doctors.
How much of your suffering—physical, psychological, and emotional—has been brought about by your own reactions to stress? More than you realize, says Roy Masters, and with this book he helps you to break your dependency on others for
your well-being. 222 pages, $9.95.

Beyond the Known
Science has long claimed that none of us is living up to his full inherent potential.
Those willing to break free from their past limitations will find a powerful assist in this book that is full of penetrating insight. 255 pages, $9.95.

The Hypnosis of Life
How is it that a stage hypnotist can take normal, well-dressed, educated people
and quickly take control of their minds? Could it be that these people are already hypnotized?
In "The Hypnosis of Life," Roy Masters, a former professional hypnotist, reveals the mysteries of our early childhood conditioning, and shows, in no uncertain terms, how hypnotic pressures and subtle suggestions affect your everyday behavior. 259 pages, $9.95.

How to Survive Your Parents
In this fascinating book, Roy Masters systematically pinpoints methods of healing family problems in a most simple way. "Forgiveness and love," says Masters, "is what most parents need more than anything in this world. Learning to forgive and love your own parents in spite of the past is the key to personal joy and happiness." 190 pages, $9.95.

Eat No Evil
Alongside America's national frenzy to control the bulging waistline is an increasing consciousness that something important is missing, and that no matter how many diets come our way, the results will be temporary and disappointing. "Eat No Evil" bypasses the typical mumbo jumbo of the "diet expert" and reveals the psychology behind our fascination with food.127 pages, $9.95

The Secret Power of Words
Under the influence of family and peer pressure, persuasive arguments can make you doubt what you feel and believe. Unfortunately, all too often this oversensitivity may cause you to depend on others to make decisions for you, which makes life progressively more difficult and confusing. This book will help you regain lost self-confidence by bringing to light the subtle personality weaknesses that allow other people to hurt and take advantage of you. 213 pages, $9.95.

The Adam & Eve Sindrome
With the rate of divorce and family breakdown so high, how can a man or woman be assured of finding the right mate and avoiding the pain and suffering caused by marital failure? "The Adam & Eve Sindrome" is a definitive guide to what, why, and how to recognize, understand, and avoid the mistakes that lead to broken hearts, homes, and health. 266 pages, $9.95.

To order Toll Free call: 1-800-877-3227 during regular business hours.

For those of you who have never attended one of Roy Masters' seminars, this is an excellent opportunity to meet like-minded people and discover a new and joyous way of life.

No one can afford to be mentally or physically unhealthy. Recent statistics show that 54 million Americans smoke cigarettes, more than 18 million are alcoholics, and over 30% of all Americans are overweight. Stress is blamed for everything from job burnout to divorce to premature death. Failure to cope with stress places an unnatural strain on the individual, both mentally and physically. Roy Masters' seminars work on a very simple principle which, when understood, can convert the stress of life to serve as a strengthening catalyst for growth and positive change.

"Right on target! Roy Masters revitalizes ageless wisdom. For many, one hour with Roy Masters will be more beneficial than years of traditional therapy."

—Clancy D. Mackenzie
Director of Philadelphia Psychiatric
Consultation Service

How many times have you unwittingly compounded a problem by being upset or angry? And how many times have you reflected back upon an argument or misunderstanding and wished that you had kept your cool? Without realizing it, the very moment you respond to stress (any kind of pressure) you are thrown off balance and you begin to deal with problems and situations from a reactive attitude. In this state of mind you become an extension of the pressure source and lose control. The more you react emotionally, the more guilty and depressed you feel, until you just wish you could shut out the world and pretend that the pressures and problems didn't exist. But wishing or pretending doesn't solve anything. In this state of mind, you are setting yourself up to be even more vulnerable to the stresses that you do not want to, or know how to, face.

Avoiding stress is what people do when they don't know how to face it properly, but sooner or later you simply have to face stress and conquer it or become its victim. If you smoke, drink, take tranquilizers or any mood controlling drugs, if you are subject to anxiety, guilt, or depression, it's time to face the culprit. Reacting with anger to life's many stresses creates a chain reaction of emotions that are responsible for your lack of self control. Roy Masters' books, radio program, instructional cassettes, and seminars will arm you with the understanding and awareness of how to deal with myriad daily pressures and show you how to maintain control over the most difficult situations. Through practicing the simple observation-concentration exercise taught by Roy Masters, you will experience a profound change in your relationship to stress and discover the rewards of overcoming your reactions to the pressures that were once overwhelming.

In order to manage stress effectively you must first see that your reactions to everyday experiences are allowing them to exert a subtle hypnotic influence upon you. Here is how it works. Virtually everyone is oversensitive to certain types of people and places, and as a result experiences discomfort and anxiety. As you become emotional you lose *awareness*, and this is the basis of your dilemma. Each negative reaction erodes your willingness to deal with problems or obstacles, and lowers your defenses until your secret personality weaknesses are exposed, inviting people to take advantage of you. Ultimately, these unconscious and unmanageable character weaknesses form the root of your negative reactions to stress. Once off balance, you act irrationally. Under the spell of emotion you do and say things you would normally suppress. In essence, you are not yourself.

The secret to unlimited patience, courage, and self-control is learning how to stop reacting to simple stresses. Anger produced by stress causes the unbearable internal tensions that lead to many illnesses and is largely responsible for tension headaches, migraines, ulcers, hypertension, colitis, asthma, and many other illnesses that can be linked to negative emotions. Like most symptoms, emotional anxiety is a warning that something is wrong, an internal indicator prompting you to look at the actual cause of the problems. Roy Masters' various materials show you how to dissect a problem objectively right down to the actual causative mechanisms They teach how to stay calm and aware under pressure and show you how to become the person you really want to be.

If you have struggled with negative emotions, such as guilt, or anxiety, and if you have tried in vain to find the answers to why and how to overcome them, Roy Masters is going to help your whole life take on a positive new perspective. Over the years Roy's seminars have helped change literally thousands of peoples' lives for the better. Now you can finally learn how to control your negative emotional responses, and conquer emotional conflict, guilt, fear, and depression once and for all. At each seminar, in-depth discussions help to bring forth self-understanding that allows you to experience a new, calm way to live, and become the strong, confident person you have always wanted to be. There has never been a more effective way to learn to observe people and experiences with calm composure.

Using this powerful catalyst for positive change, you will find your emotional wounds healing as you begin to open up to the pain and fear that you have suppressed for so long. We all know that wrong emotional response can cause misery and unhappiness, but learning how to respond correctly can restore us to happiness, health, and better relations with one another. Unimpeded by the debilitating effects of negative emotions, the body tends toward health and the mind toward happiness, peace, and fulfilling relationships. For dates of upcoming seminars call (800) 877-3227.

New Materials by Roy Masters
Tape & Lecture of the month

For those of you that are unable to hear the radio program regularly, we offer the "Tape of the Month." Each month throughout the year you will receive a 90-minute cassette tape (12 in all) featuring the very best of each month's discussions and commentary from Roy's daily radio show. The subjects and discussions are personally selected by Roy Masters. The cost for a one-year subscription—$100, or $10 per individual tape. Please add $12 for first class postage.

And now there is the lecture of the month. Each month Roy Masters conducts a series of evening lectures on a variety of important topics ranging from man/woman relationships to the meaning of life. For those of you that are unable to attend these valuable and enriching lectures this is a wonderful way to keep in touch with Roy's insights and discoveries. The cost for a one-year subscription—$100, or $10 per individual tape. Please add $12 for first class postage.

Newest lecture and seminar tapes by Roy Masters

1. Conquering Anger (Sept. 1990—90 min./$10)
2. The Mystery of Christ on the Cross (Sept. 1990—90 min./$10)
3. Sex and Self-respect—Roy Masters and Terry Mathews, Director of Brighton Academy (Sept. 1990—90 min./$10)
4. Understanding Original Sin (Sept. 1990—series of five tapes 60 minutes each./$10 each tape or $40 for the set of five)
5. Letting go of Childhood Molestation—WARNING! Do not play for children or while driving. Recorded at 1990 Christmas Seminar at Tall Timber Ranch. (Two 90-min. tapes/$20)
6. The Power of Loving Dad—(Christmas Seminar 1990, 90 min./$10)
7. The Secret Power of Values (January 1991, 90 min./$10)
8. Why Not Sex Before Marriage? (#5736/90 min./$10)
9. Solving Family Problems (#5737 90 min./$10)
10. Commonsense Christianity: Perfecting the Soul (#5738 /90 min./$10)
11. What They're Not Telling You About Teenage Sex (#5735/90 min./$10)
12. Stress-free Seminar—tapes 1 thru 6 (December 1989/90 min. Each tape $10 or all 6 for $50)
13. Roy Masters' newest book: Surviving the Comfort Zone—Quality Paperback, $12.95,

(Please add $1.50 for postage and handling to book and tape orders.)

Brand new! Commonsense Christianity

Roy Masters recently began a dynamic new series of lectures on a topic that he has never before devoted his full attention to. He calls it the "Commonsense Christianity" series. These 90-minute lectures delve into aspects of Bible understanding that we all are missing. These audio cassette tapes are available individually at a cost of $10 per tape or at a special discounted price for the 3-part series for only $20. please add $3 postage and handling for the set and $1.50 for each separate single tape that you order.

Individual Commonsense Christianity tapes $10 each

"Origin and Destiny" #5745—2/17/91
"The key to success" # 5750— 2/21/91
"What it means to be saved" #5751—2/24/91
"What does a woman really want?" #5755—2/28/91
"The mystery of love through faith" #5756—3/3/91
"Uncovering the root of addiction" #5764—3/7/91
"The Lord's prayer" #5765 REC ON 3/10/91 (Video)
"Addiction: Dealing with the cause" #5770—3/14/91 (Video)
"Judge not, lest ye be judged" #5777—3/17/91 (Video)
"None come to the father except by me" #5783—3/24/91 (Video)

COMMONSENSE CHRISTIANITY, PART I $20
 1. Secret power of words
 2. Origin & Destiny
 3. What it really means to be saved

COMMONSENSE CHRISTIANITY, PART II $20
 1. What does a woman really want?
 2. The mystery of love through faith
 3. The Lord's prayer

SPECIAL PACKAGE ON ADDICTION $20
Becoming free from
self-destructive habits
 1. Uncovering the root
of addiction
 2. Addiction: Dealing with the cause
 3. Overcoming alcohol and drug addiction through observation

+ AVAILABLE ON VHS CASSETTE, 60 MIN./$20

Meditation tapes

 1. Classic meditation—The original meditation issued over 35 years ago, this down-to-basics observation exercise is back by popular demand. $15

 2. The "Stress-free System" Roy Masters' latest version of the observation exercise brought up to date to help you deal with today's high pressure world. 3 cassette tapes only: $39.95. With the book "How Your Mind Can Keep You Well" $49.95

 3. "The Science of Controlling Stress" Three concentration exercises on different levels of difficulty: Pain, stress, and fear.
60 min each, $49.95.

For fastest service call: 1-800-877-3227
Visa & Mastercard orders only please.